AMBUSH HOUSE

KURT STEEL

NEW YORK
HARCOURT, BRACE AND COMPANY

FOR

K'EN AND HER NANA

AMBUSH HOUSE

1

HENRY HYER stood at the window looking down into Bank Street's twilit commerce. In the dim light of a street lamp, his bland good-natured face showed the strain of a vigil approaching some climax. Anxious, intent, he studied closely every pedestrian approaching from the street end.

The room at Hyer's back was silent, deeply shadowed. It was a long second-floor room, extending unbroken to the garden windows at the rear of the house. These windows, like the one at which Hyer stood, were open. Their white curtains moved gently in the April breeze. A robin chirruped once from a hidden ailanthus tree, and a lawn mower whirred as Hyer's neighbor Burke indulged a fond illusion in the skiff-sized back yard next door.

The telephone rang. Hyer wheeled, stumbled, knocked the phone to the floor. Muttering, he found the switch of a bronze-shaded lamp on a desk between the two windows, and in its sudden brilliance grappled for the telephone cord.

He said, "Hello!" sharply. Then in a politer tone, "Oh, no thank y— I mean, no not yet. . . . Don't worry." He hung up.

Turning again to the window, Hyer drew a long breath. He stiffened, rising on the balls of his feet like a fighter—a well-tailored fighter, a middleweight perhaps, graduated unmarked from rosined canvas to some more suave and affluent trade area, but still lean, compact, narrow-hipped.

"Boss."

Hyer blew out his breath and whirled. He said, "Oh, are you still there?"

Midway down the long room stood a fat squat colored man, wearing an immaculate spinnaker-like coat and a global glistening expression of alarm as he watched his employer. "Who was that, boss?"

"Teacher again."

Alarm nestled even deeper among the folds of Jonah Hastie's ebon face, glittered brightly in his wide eyes, and set his triple chins to quivering.

Hyer resumed his post at the window. Again the room was silent.

It was a pleasant room, seen now in the glow from
the bronze-shaded lamp, spacious, high-ceilinged, cool,
and having, even in shadow, the air of a place comfortably and variously lived in.

The windows, both front and back, extended from
floor to ceiling and were framed in russet drapes. The
desk which bore the bronze lamp was wide and deep,
the carving of its time-tempered mahogany glowing
softly where the light fell.

At the left near a door was a deep couch of russet
leather and beyond the desk, against a wall of books,
was a leather armchair of forest green.

Midway of its length, about where Jonah stood, the
room changed character subtly. Here was a grand piano,
and opposite the piano was a couch which fronted a
marble fireplace. Beyond the fireplace, half-hidden in
shadow, stood a doll's house as high as a little girl.

Unlike most doll's houses, this was not an unimagina-
tive white clapboard dwelling from some stereotyped
Lilliputian suburb. It was a town house, its brownstone
front complete to steps, stoop, and iron-railinged area-
way. It was, indeed, a copy of the very house in which
it stood; and on the second floor of the doll's house could
be found a room that was part study, part living room—
part male-utilitarian, part little-girl, and yet quite pleasantly a whole.

The doorbell rang.

Hyer stiffened.

Jonah murmured, "Oh, oh, bad news sure."

"Don't stand there."

"Maybe *you* better go, boss."

"Answer that door," Hyer said grimly. "I'll wait here."

Jonah swallowed, stilled two of his oscillant chins, and shuffled to the door. Hyer could hear him descending to the hallway below.

Hyer braced himself against the broad mahogany desk. He took a cigarette from his case, saw his hand tremble, and flicked the cigarette angrily through a window.

From below came a murmur of voices. Hyer inhaled sharply, held his breath while an agony of apprehension showed in his face. Then, as he listened, the alarm vanished. His shoulders sagged. He touched his forehead and drew out a handkerchief.

As a running step sounded on the stairs, Hyer grinned. The handkerchief faltered as he drew it down his face. He squinted upward into the shadow and murmured, "Thanks . . ."

The doorknob turned. The door swung inward slowly, came to rest a third of the way open. At shoulder height the brim of a hat showed. Eighteen inches below it, a small crown of jet-black hair appeared. Two button-bright eyes peered cautiously around the edge of the door, caught sight of Hyer, and withdrew in haste. The elevated hat disappeared.

"Come here," Hyer said sternly.

The door swung slowly through the remainder of its arc.

On the threshold stood a little girl of nine. Her glossy

black hair hung straight as an Indian's to her shoulders. This, with the sharp-edged line of bangs across her forehead and the innocence of her wide-eyed gaze, gave to the child's oval face an almost angelic pallor and purity. She had a slender wiry body and straight thin arms and legs. Under an open blue coat there showed a jumper of gray and a white bodice.

Hyer lifted an eyebrow. "Angelica, where have you been?"

Angelica came into the room. She smiled. "At school, *tío mío.*"

"An-*gel*-ica!"

Pause.

"Oh," Angelica said in a small voice.

"Where have you been?"

Angelica's mouth puckered and a frown appeared.

Hyer, watching a familiar portent of disaster, slipped off the corner of the desk and said hastily, "All right, all right. Better get right at your pract—"

"But you want to know where I am being," Angelica protested.

"In English, yes."

"*No tengo,*" she began regretfully, "*la palabra inglesa—*"

"Angelica!"

The doorbell rang.

Her distress was pitiable. "*Pero es verdad, tío mío. No tengo la palabra inglesa para . . .*" Angelica's voice trailed off disconsolately. Her black eyes were wide— and impish.

For a moment the man and the little girl stubbornly faced each other. But to the struggle there could be only one outcome. Experience had taught Hyer that he might as easily pry secrets from a pitcher's ears as one word of English from this small exiled Madrileña when a change of subject served her purpose.

Hyer sighed. He reached for a well-thumbed Spanish-English dictionary on his desk. "Well, what is it?"

A buzzer sounded. Jonah's voice came from a speaker under the desk. "Man anna lady to see you, boss."

Angelica said sweetly, "I was *en el museo de historia natural.*"

Hyer sat at the desk, opened the dictionary with his left hand, absently depressed a switch. "Slower," he said to Angelica.

"Somebody—" Jonah repeated deliberately, "to— see—"

"Not you," Hyer snapped. "What's the word? Quick."

"What word, boss?"

Angelica said, "*Museo—*"

"Hold it." Hyer riffled the pages of the dictionary.

"What'll I tell'm, boss?" Jonah asked.

"Museum!" Hyer announced, looking up from the dictionary.

"Sure I seen'm," Jonah said in disgust. "You think—?"

"All right, Jonah. They can come up." Hyer closed the book. He took his finger from the speaker switch. "As for you, Miss Ananias, you get upstairs and start your homework. If you ever— Wait a minute," he com-

manded as Angelica turned demurely to leave. "Come
here."

When the child stood before him, Hyer cupped his
hand about the nape of her neck under the straight
black hair. With his thumb and forefinger, he lifted her
chin. "Honey," he said softly, "don't skip school again
without telling—"

"But I get so—*cómo se dice*—"

"Bored?"

Angelica nodded.

"Next time, baby, when it gets too bad, you tell me.
I know a lot of better places we could go on an' April
afternoon. Now run along. I've got company." He spun
Angelica about, patted her flat little *derrière*, and gave
her a push.

At the door she looked back. "What places, *tío
mío?*"

"Get out. Before I remember I promised teacher to
discipline you."

She laughed, ran out of the room and up the stairs
to the third floor.

There was a shuffling step in the hallway, a puffing,
and Jonah swung open the door with a flourish. "Miss
Madeira Thayer," Jonah said formally, "*an'* Mist' Pedro
Vicente Cordero."

Hyer blinked. "Not more Spanish," he murmured.

Jonah stood back. A young woman entered the room
followed by a tall broad-shouldered man of thirty-five
or six with black eyes, red hair, and a thick red spade
beard.

Hyer bowed. "*Señorita y señor, buenas noches.*"

White teeth showed against the red beard. "*Buenas noches, señor.*"

Madeira Thayer smiled. "Good evening, Mr. Hyer." She had a pleasant smile. But there was a tightness about her lips, and a cool intent appraisal in the glance she gave Hyer.

She appeared to be in her early twenties. There was a crisp decisive quality about her, a promise of spirit in her level dark eyes, irony lurking at the corner of her mouth. In gray tweed suit and neat blue fusillier's cap she was lithe, erect, not tall—she came barely to the shoulder of the big man with her—but there was something commanding in the way she stood before Hyer and said, "I want to hire you."

Looking at her, listening to the forthright announcement, Hyer let amusement show in his bland face. Then, abruptly, the amusement vanished. His eyes grew still, and something like incredulity appeared in them briefly. He turned to Cordero. "Won't you sit down?" But as if drawn against his will, his glance returned to the girl.

Cordero touched her elbow and bowed her to the russet couch. He waited, and then sat beside her. He said, "We need the professional help of a man like yourself, Hyer." His black eyes (they were, Hyer noted with astonishment, quite as black as Angelica's) were bright and probing.

"I want you to find a man," Madeira Thayer said crisply.

Hyer started to speak, looked at her with sharp unbelief, turned and sought a leather cigarette case on the desk as though to bridge a difficult moment.

As he faced about again, the door opened. Angelica entered. At sight of Hyer's visitors, she halted in apparent confusion. The confusion, Hyer noticed with amusement, did not prevent her black eyes from making a swift and detailed inspection of the two callers.

Hyer said gently, "Of course, Angelica, how were *you* to know anybody was here?"

She regarded him innocently. "*Perdona, Tío Enrique. Volveré cuando—*"

"*No, no hagas caso,*" Madeira said, smiling.

At the blank amazement that showed in Angelica's face, Hyer chuckled: "Make it as hard as you like, honey. I've got something better than a dictionary this time."

Cordero's white teeth flashed. "*Qué quieres, pequeñita?*"

This double sally in her native tongue was too much for Angelica. She grew red under Hyer's amusement, backed a step uncertainly, curtsied, and fled.

Cordero threw back his head and laughed. His laughter filled the long room, set the piano in the shadows humming.

"Your daughter, Mr. Hyer?" Madeira asked.

"No. She was a fee."

"A fee?"

"Her guardian," Hyer explained, "was a client of mine. I—well, I had some bad luck with him. His estate

didn't amount to enough to pay my bill. So I took it
out in trade. Angelica was the trade. She was born in
Madrid. The bombs got the rest of her family, except
for a brother in Montevideo."

"Oh, and you adopted her when her guardian died?"

"As a hobby," Hyer confessed, "it turned out to be
expensive." His glance wandered down the remodeled
room, rested on the massive piano, the doll's house. He
winced. "First a governess. That meant more room. I'd
lived here on this one floor for ten years and been comfortable. So I rented another floor. Then we had to have
more help, so I hired the minstrel Santa Claus who let
you in. Then *he* needed more room. By then I saw how
things were going, so to keep the overhead down I simply bought the house."

Cordero laughed. "And started remodeling?"

Hyer said brightly, "So you see how it is. I'm afraid
I can't do anything for you, Miss Thayer." He spoke
rapidly, like a man anxious to end something.

"But I don't see."

"I've developed expensive habits, Miss Thayer."

"What has that to do with—?"

"How much is it worth to you to find this man?"

Madeira Thayer stared at him curiously. "We were
told, of course, that you were accustomed to large fees."

"Your fee will be guaranteed, Hyer," Cordero said.
"If you will name a figure . . ."

Hyer looked at Madeira. The baffled unbelief reappeared. He turned to Cordero, seemed to be avoiding

the girl's eyes with an effort. He said, "One hundred thousand dollars."

Madeira Thayer stood up. She said with spirit: "You're quite an experience, Mr. Hyer. Good-by." She went swiftly out of the room.

Cordero took out a card. He handed it to Hyer with an ironical light in his black eyes. "If you should change your mind, Mr. Hyer—or revise your price list . . . *Hasta luego.*"

As Jonah let the visitors out downstairs, Angelica came into the room again. Hyer was standing at the window. Angelica went to stand beside him. Her hand slipped hesitantly into his.

"I'm sorry, *tío mío.* About the school, I mean."

Hyer looked down at her. His eyes were troubled. "Don't do it again, honey."

"Never!"

"Oh, oh," Hyer cautioned. "What about exaggerating?"

She grinned slowly. "I try, I mean."

Hyer nodded. "That's safer."

For a moment there was silence. A cab door slammed. Hyer turned from the window.

"Why won't you help the Señorita Thayer, Tío Hank?" the little girl asked softly.

Hyer dropped into the desk chair. He stared absently at the shadowy piano.

"*Es una muchacha muy simpática,*" Angelica murmured.

The cab drove away.

Hyer drew the little girl into his arm. He pinched
her ear, said: "Look what happened to me the last time
I got mixed up in a Spanish— What was that?" he asked,
frowning.

"*Pero es tambien una muchacha muy hermosa.*"

Absently Hyer reached for the dictionary. His hand
halted in mid-career. He looked pleased. "*Hermosa—
hermosa*—'beautiful.' I'm learning Spanish, honey."

"She is, *verdad*. Then you will help her?" Angelica
asked eagerly.

"No, baby."

"But why? Why, Tío Hank?"

Hyer hesitated. He smiled at her, tweaked her nose.
"Honey, it wouldn't pay the light bill for a week.
Money, *dinero, dinero*. We've got to think of that, An-
gelica."

Angelica sighed. "Always, *Tío Enrique?*"

"Always."

Darkness deepened in the street. From belowstairs
came the remote clatter of pans as Jonah worked in the
basement kitchen.

Angelica said softly: "But the real reason, Tío Hank—
It is not *dinero*, no?"

Hyer gave a start. "The real reason?"

"You do not like the Señorita Thayer," Angelica
accused.

For a moment, Hyer did not answer. Then he said,
"And you don't like Monty Woolley, Angelica."

Her lips tightened. She shook her head slowly. "No,
Tío Hank. It is only that to see him in the play. . . . I

look and remember my grandpapa—*mi muy querido abuelo*—who is dead." She looked hard at Hyer, comprehending. "And so the Señorita Thayer—you look at her and remember some other . . . ?"

Hyer nodded. He smoothed her black hair.

"And she is dead, too, Tío Hank?" softly.

"She is dead, Angelica. There was a train wreck."

The doorbell rang.

Hyer got up quickly. He said: "There's Miss Glover home from her sister's in the Bronx. We'll both be better off if you're practicing when she comes in. Hurry."

Hand in hand, they ran toward the piano.

2

BUT it was not Angelica's governess. When formalities were over and Angelica had been dispatched to the third floor again, Hyer found himself once more favored with two callers.

"Like Old Home Week," he said hospitably. "What would you gentlemen like to drink?"

The younger of the two men seated on the couch said, "Nothing, thank you." He was a solid man with a squarish florid face, narrow eyes, thin straight lips, light hair parted in the middle, and square blunt-fingered hands. His gray suit was of an expensive weave, tailored appropriately.

16

"You?" Hyer asked of the other.

"Nothing for him, either." The florid-faced man spoke in an offhand manner as if the wishes of his companion were of no importance.

Hyer lifted an eyebrow. Ignoring the spokesman, he said genially to his second visitor, "You look like a bourbon man to me."

The man's pale eyes brightened. "Why, yes, I'd thank you for a spot." He had a lank, wasted look. His suit, obviously a hand-me-down, hung loosely from his gaunt shoulders, but failed to cover his bony ankles and reddened wrists. Despite this handicap, there was about him a trim, shipshape air. His thinning gray hair was neatly brushed back from bony temples. His cheeks, sunken as if he had recently undergone an illness, were smooth-shaven, his gray mustache was neatly clipped.

"My name," the first man said brusquely as Hyer directed Jonah to bring whisky, "is Braun. Albert Braun." He watched Jonah bend, puffing, to open a cabinet, then turned to Hyer and asked bluntly, "What did Miss Thayer ask you to do?"

Hyer said, "She wants the Lizzie Borden thing settled."

Braun's florid face grew a shade darker. "Whatever it was, Hyer, my advice to you is to—"

"Here's the bourbon," Hyer said brightly as Jonah came from the cabinet. "Soda, Mr.—?"

The lank visitor edged forward on the couch. His Adam's apple worked. "My name's Klim. Eben Klim. I'll take it straight, if you don't mind." He clutched the edge of the couch with his left hand, set his hat on the floor carefully, and reached for the glass which Jonah held out. "Thank you—boy."

Jonah blinked, looked at Hyer, went to the door muttering.

Braun was watching Hyer. The man's momentary pique had passed. His eyes narrowed suddenly as if he had come to a decision. He said shortly, "All right, Klim, you can go now."

Color showed in the other's sunken cheeks. "I've got as much right—"

"You heard me."

Klim's Adam's apple rose and dropped. He looked at Hyer. Hyer winked. Klim cleared his throat, stood up. To Braun he said, "If you don't let me in on . . ." His voice rose and trailed away uncertainly.

Hyer said, "Nice knowing you, Mr. Klim. Drop in when you're in the neighborhood. Jonah," he called, "show Mr. Klim out."

Neither Braun nor Hyer spoke until they heard the front door close on the sped guest.

"Shabby way to treat him after what he did for you," Hyer observed. He sat down at the desk.

"How do you know what he did?" Braun asked sharply.

"You didn't open a classified directory and put your finger on my name."

"No."

"Klim was following the Thayer girl for you, wasn't

he?" Hyer asked. "When she came here, he phoned you."

Braun moved his hand impatiently. "Whatever she offered you, Hyer, my advice—"

"That," Hyer said quietly, "is why I was willing to let you stay and talk. People with advice for me . . . interest me." His eyes were unfriendly. "Go on."

"Don't have anything to do with Madeira Thayer."

Hyer studied the other man. His hand slipped below the desk top.

In a moment Jonah's voice came from the speaker. "Yes, boss. You ring?"

"Call Miss Thayer for me," Hyer said, "and tell her I'll take her case after all. Tell her I've had a talk with a Mr. Braun."

"Yes, boss. You still want dinner at seb'm."

"For Angelica, yes." Hyer eyed Braun. "I'm going out and see a Señor Cordero about a—"

"Wait a minute," Braun broke in hastily.

"What's that, boss?"

"Nothing. Come to think of it, I'll call Miss Thayer myself." Hyer reached for the telephone.

"All right," Braun confessed. "I misjudged you."

"And I misjudged you," Hyer said slowly. He pushed the phone away. "You're softer than I took you for. I guess it's your face."

Braun reddened. He stood up. "If you'd been willing to listen to me, Hyer—"

"*Es una muchacha muy simpática, verdad?*" Hyer asked. "Good night, Mr. Braun."

He stood at the window, watched the other man get into his car and drive away. His manner at the moment was that of a man who, having made a difficult decision, is yet reluctant to set out.

A few minutes before seven Hyer left the house and walked briskly toward a cab rank. Within twenty paces he knew he was being followed. He turned a corner, stopped, waited. Eben Klim, hastening around the corner, collided with him.

"Hello," Hyer said affably.

Klim's Adam's apple bobbed. "You give me a start, Mr. Hyer."

Hyer took the lank visitor by the arm, fell into step with him. "Let's both cross Braun up," he suggested amiably. He waited, was aware of Klim's sudden discomfort. "All he's done is try to push us both around." Again Hyer waited. "Gives us a common interest in him, doesn't it?"

Klim moved his bony shoulder uneasily and withdrew his arm from Hyer's grasp. "Still, I don't know, Mr. Hyer."

"Come in here and let's talk about it." Hyer guided Klim, unresistant, into a bar. They went to the back of the room, out of earshot of a small group near the door.

When the bartender had come and gone, Hyer lifted his glass. "Looking at you."

Klim poured whisky eagerly past his bobbing Adam's apple, blinked, and drew a breath. His pale eyes were brighter. "So you think Mr. Braun's trying to cut me out of my share in finding . . . the watch?"

"Look how he got rid of you." Hyer watched the struggle in Klim's thin face. "Confidentially, how much did he offer you to get him the . . . you know, the watch?"

Klim plucked at his mouth with a nervous hand and looked away. "A hundred dollars."

"A hundred? Suppose I were to say he offered me *five*, Klim."

Klim's pale eyes hardened. A furious red flowed into his thin cheeks. "Why, the—"

"Why don't you tell me what you know, Klim, and I'll see whether it checks with what he told me."

Klim's Adam's apple moved. Then caution reawakened. "Still, you being a detective—"

"What have *you* got to hide?"

"Nothing," Klim said promptly. "Not a thing, Mr. Hyer."

"I tell you what," Hyer said. "I'll give you two hundred and fifty for the watch. That's better than Braun's offer. How about it?"

Cupidity gleamed in Klim's washed-out eyes. "All right, Mr. Hyer. What do you want to know?"

"Run over the whole story," Hyer said casually. "I'll pick out what I want as we go along."

"Well, I guess Mr. Braun told you I was second engineer on the *Fort Moore*. I'd signed on in Halifax and we'd been down below the bulge for a load of hides. And how them hides did stink—not proper cured or something. Well, anyway, at Trinidad two passengers come aboard. One of 'em called himself Reed Mallory

—had a passport and everything he did—but Mr. Braun says his real name was something else, I don't know. He was fairly young, 'bout your own age I'd guess, maybe thirty-five, six. The thing made you notice him though was his face. That's how Braun knew who he was when I described Reed to Braun down there in that hospital in Charleston. (We'd been rescued by then, you see, and Reed had already robbed the hospital and got away.)"

"Faces," Hyer said, "come in all shapes."

Klim's thin shoulders twitched. "You never see one like Reed's, Mr. Hyer. Made a man's skin creep. Like somebody'd took a piece out o' one cheek and then all squooged it up and sewed it that way. Nineteen days I spent on a raft with that face." Klim shuddered. "I'd thank you for another drink, I guess."

Presently the engineer continued. "The other passenger, his name was John Thayer. He was older'n Reed. A fellow 'bout middle heighth, quiet, he didn't talk much. He had a streak of white in his hair. I guess he'd seen Reed before—knew him by sight, that is, but not by name. Leastwise he called him Mallory, but Braun says that wasn't Reed's real name.

"Well, anyway, there we was—two passengers and a short-handed crew slogging along som'eres off the Bahamas when we hit a mine that'd floated in from God knows where. Touched her off amidships, it did, right where her rotten plates was weakest. The boilers let go and tore her open like a paper sack.

"It was just sundown and I happened to be standing

aft talking to the two passengers. The three of us was blowed square end over end into the water quite a piece from where the *Moore* was already settling. Lucky she was a coal-burner and we didn't have no oil to fight.

"Anyway, I found something to hang on to and it was a raft. Seems the three of us landed pretty close together, because I hadn't more'n pulled myself up on the raft when I see somebody floundering and it's Reed with his ugly face. I pulled him up and he began taking on something terrible about where was Thayer.

"The water was full of crates and gear and wreckage, and at first it didn't look like another living soul was left. But just then we see a little kind of light and it's the white streak in Thayer's hair. Well, we got him aboard and we could see he was bad hurt. Next morning he was worse and I figured if we wasn't picked up pretty quick he'd be a goner.

"And that's what happened. Thayer lasted three days. Getting weaker and weaker and Reed taking care of 'im like he was a trained nurse—Reed, I mean. Anyway, Thayer died along toward evening of the third day.

"But before he died, Thayer give Reed something. They tried to keep it private, not letting me in on what they was doing. But you might's well try to hide your hat on a concrete floor as keep anything secret on a raft. Anyway, after we'd give Thayer a Christian burial, I put it up to Reed. 'We go halvers on whatever you got,' I told him. 'What is it?'

"For a while Reed pretended he didn't know what I was talking about. He held out for a couple days. Then

he give in. It was pretty bad by that time. Burned to a
crisp we were by the sun and our tongues so swole up
we could only mumble. Finally Reed said all right,
Thayer had give him his watch.

"Well, Reed showed me the watch, and it wasn't
much at that. Just an ordinary gold watch, kind o' old-
fashioned and thicker'n you see 'm nowadays. Reed said
Thayer'd asked him to take the watch to his daughter
in New York if he ever got rescued.

"Well, we wasn't thinking much about watches or
anything else by that time. Everything was kind of
crazy and yellowlike and we was both out of our heads
a good piece of the time. Finally they picked us up and
took us in to Charleston, where we woke up in hospital beds one day.

"Reed, bein' younger and tougher'n me, he got his
strength back quicker." Klim's mouth twitched, and remembered anger lighted his eyes. "That is, Reed got
his strength back enough to sneak out one night—after
laying a watchman cold and robbing a till in the hospital.

"It was just next day that Mr. Braun showed up. He'd
seen a paragraph in a New York paper about our being picked up, and he'd made the trip down to Charleston, thinking one of us might be Thayer. I told him no,
Thayer had died, and I described Reed to him—Reed
who'd got away to God knows where by that time with
the watch and the hospital's cash and a warrant out for
him.

"Well, when I described Reed, Braun got all excited.

And when I told him about Thayer's watch, I thought he'd throw a fit. Anyway, the upshot was he paid my way back to New York because, knowing Reed by sight the way I did, maybe I could help him find Reed.

"So what he did was have me watch a big apartment house up in Highbridge—seems Reed's brother lives in that house, and Braun figured Reed might turn up there."

"Did he?"

"Why, no, sir, Mr. Hyer," Klim said promptly, a shade too promptly. "No, sir, he never did that."

Hyer started to ask a question, shrugged. "All right, we won't rush things. When you feel chapter two coming on, drop in and see me."

Presently they walked out. As they reached the sidewalk, Hyer said casually, "By the way, you can use an advance on that two hundred and fifty, maybe."

"I'm stony," Klim confessed.

Hyer took a $20 bill from his wallet. "This is on account. We'll work out the balance later."

Klim's Adam's apple worked as his thin fingers took the money. Gratitude swept the last traces of suspicion from his eyes. He mumbled, "Well, if you— All right."

A minute later, Klim hurried after Hyer, who had stepped into a cab. "There's something else," Klim said hastily through the cab window. "Something I never told Mr. Braun."

"What?"

"There was a picture in the back of that watch," Klim said in a low voice. "It was the picture of a girl. Reed showed it to me when he was— Well, from the way he acted, I guess he musta been a little outta his head."

"Why, Klim?"

"He showed me the picture of this girl—"

"Ever see the girl?" Hyer asked.

Klim shook his head. "Pretty she was, but just a young girl, maybe fifteen, sixteen—"

"What did Reed say?"

"Reed said," Klim answered, his voice still lower, "Reed said, 'Klim, I'm going to find this girl if it's the last thing I do.' "

"Honest chap."

"Reed said," Klim whispered, " 'I'm going to find her if it takes the rest of my life—*because I'm going to kill her!* ' "

3

A LITTLE after ten that night, Henry Hyer found himself, to his surprise, riding north from the city along River Parkway. Beside him at the wheel sat Pedro Vicente Cordero of the red beard and the jovial laugh. Cordero was not laughing now. He was explaining something to Hyer, explaining it carefully and slowly as if it were important that Hyer miss no smallest detail.

"On last Friday afternoon," Cordero was saying, "a Mr. Braun came to Madeira." His American inflection was without flaw save for a tendency to treat certain vowels with Latin tenderness.

27

"Braun?" Hyer asked. "Not Charley Braun of the *Examiner?*"

"No, this is—" Cordero coughed. "I've no idea what his first name is."

"Charley Braun's a friend of mine," Hyer explained easily. "He gets around a good deal and picks up all sorts of things. I thought maybe—" He moved his hand vaguely and looked out at the moon-drenched meadow they were passing.

Cordero cleared his throat. "Mr. Braun visited Madeira at her office at the Exporters Trust Company. Madeira had never seen him before. She had no idea how he found her. Anyway, here is what Braun told Madeira." Cordero paused. "Braun said her father had been on his way to North America from Trinidad—"

"Something she didn't know?" Hyer asked in surprise.

"Yes. She had expected her father some time soon, but she did not know he had started. Braun told her— you can imagine how the news affected a sensitive girl —that her father had been aboard a freighter which struck a floating mine and sank."

"That's too bad," Hyer said sympathetically. "And her father was killed?"

Cordero hesitated a moment. "No—not then, that is. He—according to Braun, he— That is, he seems to have been saved for a time, at least—on a life raft. But he was never rescued from the life raft," Cordero added, his voice suddenly bitter. He paused. "However," slowly, "there was a man aboard the life raft who was entrusted with a message to Madeira from her father."

"Oh, and he's the chap Miss Thayer wants to find?"

"Yes."

They ran for a few minutes beside a small stream. A train, riding the crest of an embankment beyond the stream, rushed up behind them, roared past, and drew ahead.

"How did Braun know all this?" Hyer asked.

"He would not tell Madeira."

"But she believed him?"

"Wait." Cordero lifted his hand. It was a strong, sinewy hand with lively fingers. Moonlight glinted on a virile diamond. "Perhaps I should tell you something about Madeira, Mr. Hyer, so you will be in a better position to understand. And about myself. I am a Venezuelan, Mr. Hyer. I have many interests in South America, but during the Gómez regime I found it convenient to form the habit of living abroad."

Cordero turned toward Hyer and his great laugh boomed. His teeth showed bright against the sorrel beard. "I have always had certain social convictions which—well, which unfit me for citizenship under a tyrant." He grew serious, added quickly, "With the Contreras government today, of course, things are different."

Hyer said, "Oh, yes," absently.

"John Thayer, Madeira's father, was a mining man, Hyer. He and I were close friends. For many years he

was resident engineer at one of my developments in
the Caroni country. As a matter of fact, Madeira herself grew up there—except for the years when she was
in school here in the States. Her mother died when
she was quite young. She was particularly fond of her
father." Cordero stopped, attended closely to his driving for a few moments.

"Her father," Hyer prompted, "was an engineer—"

"Yes. About eight months ago, John Thayer undertook a mission for myself and some of my North American associates. There had been rumors of tin deposits
in certain remote Venezuelan mountains near the Brit-
ish Guiana border. John Thayer was to investigate those
rumors for us—quite confidentially.

"In February—a little over two months ago—Madeira
had word from him. He had completed his work and
would presently be coming north." The diamond flashed
as Cordero moved his hand. "For some reason he preferred to make his report to us in person rather than
trust cable or mails."

"Because somebody else wanted the same information?"

Cordero laughed. "Our rivals have at times showed
themselves somewhat less than scrupulous, yes. Well,
that was the last word any of us had from John Thayer
until four days ago when Braun came to Madeira."

"You said she was working for—?"

"For the Exporters Trust Company. She had a very
responsible position despite her youth."

"Had?" Hyer asked. "*Had* a position?"

"Wait," Cordero said. "You are impetuous. Last Friday morning, Mr. Braun came to Madeira and said her father—that he was dead. He asked her whether a Reed Molloy had been in touch with her."

"Reed—*Molloy*," Hyer repeated as if memorizing the name.

"Braun told Madeira that this Reed Molloy had a brother, Decker Molloy—"

"Decker Molloy?" Hyer pivoted on one shoulder, looked at Cordero with sudden interest.

"Then you know Decker Molloy, Mr. Hyer?"

"Norcross County Prosecutor? Why, yes, we've met. Professionally. Go on."

"Ah, then you are interested?"

"I'm on more familiar ground, at least. We're on our way to see Decker Molloy in Highbridge now, are we?"

"Oh, no," swiftly. Then as if fearing he might be misunderstood, Cordero added, "Not tonight, that is. Perhaps— At any rate, Hyer, after Braun had left her, Madeira was considerably disturbed. She called me. We had dinner together Friday night. I suggested that we call on Decker Molloy and verify the story if we could.

"So Friday night after dinner we drove up here to Highbridge. Mr. Molloy was very courteous, but he could not help us. He said he had a brother Reed, and that Reed was, the last he knew, somewhere in South America. But he had not heard from him for years.

"Molloy's mother, a charming woman, came into the room at that point and overheard a bit of our conversation. She appeared greatly affected. Apparently this Reed was quite a favorite with her—and something of

a black sheep. That, Hyer, marked the beginning of
our mystery."

"Yes?"

"The next morning—last Saturday—Decker Molloy
called on Madeira at the bank."

"He'd heard from his brother? Well, coincidences
like that make you—"

"No." Cordero looked at Hyer. "I must admit, I'm
surprised to find a man with your professional reputation forming conclusions with such . . . facility."

"One of my worst habits," Hyer confessed. "Go on."

"As a matter of fact, Decker Molloy didn't mention
his brother again. He offered Madeira a position. Yes,"
Cordero said quickly, "it seemed quite as queer to Madeira at the time. But Molloy explained that the Norcross County District Attorney's office needed someone with precisely her talents to do some highly confidential investigating. Madeira tells me she laughed at
him. But Molloy was serious.

"Molloy told her they had been looking for an American girl with fluent South American Spanish, and that
she exactly fitted the specifications. He had already
spoken to the head of her department at the bank. The
bank was ready—reluctantly—to release her. The District Attorney offered to pay twice the salary she was
getting."

"And it gave her a chance to keep in touch with
Decker Molloy," Hyer observed.

"Yes. It seemed a reasonable thing to do—to accept
Molloy's offer, that is. But there was one condition."

"There always is."

"No, don't misunderstand me. What I meant was that Molloy requested Madeira not to return to her apartment in New York, but to go to a certain house in Highbridge. The things she needed—clothes and so forth—were to be packed for her and sent by messenger, but otherwise her apartment in New York was to be left undisturbed."

Hyer murmured, "Red-headed league."

"I beg your— Oh, yes, that story of Doyle's. Both Madeira and I thought of that. But anyway, to make a long story short, Madeira has been in that house for three days now without a word from anyone. Naturally we are becoming curious."

"Are you?"

"I persuaded Madeira to come to you." Cordero looked at Hyer. "After your . . . rather brusque decision this evening, I was surprised when I got home and learned you had changed your mind."

"Angelica took a liking to Miss Thayer."

"Splendid."

As they approached Highbridge, Hyer said, "How about stopping and seeing Molloy a minute?"

"Oh, I think that's hardly—"

"There's a drugstore," Hyer said, sitting up. "I can look up his address there."

"But I know his address. We visited him."

"So you did. All right, I'd like to stop and see Decker Molloy."

Cordero shook his head. "I doubt whether he will care to discuss the thing with a stranger."

"I'm not exactly a stranger. Anyway, that might be worth knowing."

Five minutes later they stopped in front of a large apartment house. Cordero was clearly critical of this strategy. "What will you ask Molloy, Hyer?"

"I'll think of something."

Hyer was thoughtful as he entered the elevator after sending his name up.

The door to 16B was opened by a youngish man with a high, studious forehead, black eyebrows to delight a cartoonist, sensitive dark eyes, and a firm straight mouth marred by a small white scar that slanted across both upper and lower lip. He wore a silk dressing robe with a Paisley pattern.

"Hello, Hyer," Decker Molloy said. "Quite a surprise to see you again." He had a pleasant courtroom baritone, and so nicely balanced was his manner that the acutest critic could not have told whether he enjoyed or resented this encounter. "Come in."

"Thanks," Hyer said, "I can't stay. I'm on a case. I wonder if you can help me."

"Perhaps." It was a masterful blending of courtesy and reserve.

"I'm looking for a girl—matter of an estate," Hyer explained. "Her name's Madeira Thayer."

"Madeira Thayer?" The baritone was perfectly modulated.

"She seems to have dropped out of sight recently,"

Hyer continued. "Somebody where she worked said you had talked to her—"

"I?" Just the right surprise.

"You never can be sure about gossip, of course. But some file clerk overheard a name that sounded like yours. Somebody else described the chap. He had your eyebrows."

Molloy smiled. The contact points of the scar slipped apart. "My cross. Must have been someone else, Hyer. Sorry. Come in and have a drink. You owe me something for that case you slipped out from under us. . . . Well, some other time, then." An acute observer might have noted relief in Molloy's manner as Hyer said good night.

When Hyer rejoined Cordero, the red-bearded Venezuelan asked eagerly, "What did he say?"

"You had it right. He never heard of Madeira Thayer."

"I'm not surprised. So you know him? Well, well."

They drove for a time along a wide avenue. Hyer lay back on his shoulder blades and watched the moon scud through arching new-budded boughs overhead. Presently they approached the center of town again. The character of the avenue changed.

Once-comfortable frame houses sat like decaying dowagers in their lawns, ignoring lighted dressmaker and mortuary signs that sprouted here and there like the fungus of a final decline.

They approached a corner which had already succumbed to the advancing commercial blight and was

now occupied by a theater with a covey of small shops
tucked into its façade. Cordero turned out of the avenue at this corner. They ran for a hundred feet past
the blank side of the theater with its exit door under
hooded lights, cleared an alley, and drew up in front
of the first house.

In the bright moonlight, the house was a solid, ugly
memento of the most eclectic Edwardian taste. Built
of undressed stone with a chunky crenelated tower at
one corner, it had something of the forbidding air of
a fortress, but was saved from consistency even in this
respect by a small square veranda and a bulging bay
with curving glass windows.

There were no lights.

"Madeira should be here," Cordero said, his voice
low in the April silence that enveloped them when the
motor stopped. "I left her here at eight-thirty and went
straight home to New York. If I'd known, Hyer, that
you had changed your mind— Well, shall we go in?"

Cordero's ring at the door was not answered at first.
He rang again. The bell sounded faintly.

Suddenly brilliant light flooded the veranda where
they stood. The door opened.

A deep bass voice said, "Hello, I didn't expect you
again toni— My God!"

The door was flung wide. Hyer was grasped firmly
by the hand and snapped across the threshold with the
abruptness of a mail sack plucked from its hook by a
flying express.

4

CORDERO followed Hyer and closed the door.

Hyer's hand and forearm were in the grasp of a short stocky woman with the build of a wrestler and small delicate features. Her hennaed hair was intricately and expensively waved, upswept from tiny, perfectly modeled ears, in each of which was an emerald clip. Her greenish eyes were bright with amazement. A triple strand of pearls set off her simple gray frock with startling effect. Metal bracelets weighted her slim, graceful wrists.

"*Henry—Hyer!*" she gasped in a throaty bass.

"Your circle of acquaintances, Hyer," Cordero observed, "seems to be—"

"Chiefly professional," Hyer broke in easily. Beneath the other man's banter he had sensed disquiet. "Della Doudy's one of the oldest members."

"For five years," Della Doudy growled, "I read the obituary notices every morning—and what does it get me? Eyestrain."

Hyer grinned. "There was always the chance I'd been dropped in a concrete mixer when nobody was looking."

"Come in, Hank. Come in and let me look at you." She towed Hyer down a long hallway between shadowy walls covered with framed clippings, cartoons, book jackets, theater programs, and an endless gallery of signed photographs.

Behind them, Cordero said, "I'll be with you in a moment."

Hyer, dragged on like a towed barge, looked over his shoulder. Cordero had stopped at a door on the right. It was a wide double door, ornately carved and set in a frame which must have been elaborate even in the dreams of the strange and tortured architect of the house. A staircase with a rococo balustrade ascended stiffly against the opposite wall.

Then Hyer's impetuous hostess drew him through a door at the end of the hall and closed it. He found himself in a large and astonishingly overfurnished living room. The room was crowded with petit-point chairs, little tables, corner cupboards laden with bric-a-brac, and a massive alabaster mantelpiece, intricately carved by some vanished genius whose piety had all but outrun his chisel.

The floor, from wall to wall, was covered with rich Oriental looming. Hyer wove his way through the deployed hazards until the maze closed in on him and he took refuge in a gilt Louis XV chair.

Della Doudy lifted her right foot, steadied herself by grasping an alabaster angel's nose, and absently scraped a match on the sole of her shoe. Despite her square solid bulk, her feet were small and shapely, her ankles neatly turned. Her hands—innocent of rings—were slender and graceful as they cupped about a cigarette. The carillon of bracelets jangled cheerfully as she shook out the match.

She said, "Well, well," squinting at Hyer through a trickle of cigarette smoke.

"Surprised, Della?"

"You can say that again." She walked over and stood in front of him. Her movements were smooth, graceful. She sat on the arm of a chair, leaned forward on her firm silk-smoothed thigh, and regarded Hyer. Her greenish eyes were wary, but when she spoke her bass voice was casual. "The last time I saw you, Henry Hyer, I hoped was the last time I saw you."

"Hospitable as always," Hyer observed.

Della sighed. "If it hadn't been for you, I'd still have one of the smartest layouts in New York."

"If you hadn't made the mistake of clipping a client of mine," Hyer agreed, "you might."

Della shrugged. "Mistakes will happen." She stood

up, walked to another chair, and sat again—again leaning forward. "What brings you here, Hank?"

"Still doing errands for courthouse boys on the side,
I see," Hyer said.

Della looked blank. She drew on her cigarette, ex-
haled slowly, and frowned. "I don't get it."

"Decker Molloy a friend of yours, Della?"

"Decker Molloy?" She shook her head quickly. "No,
Hank. I'm strictly Miss Little Private Citizen up here."

"Who made arrangements for your roomer?"

Again Della frowned. "You mean Miss Thayer? Why,
she did, Hank. She did herself. Miss Thayer rang the
bell last Saturday and asked did I know where she might
get a room for a few days and— Well, I don't take in
roomers as you might imagine, Hank, but Miss Thayer
seemed like such a nice kid and— Well, you know how
it is, Hank, living by yourself you get a little wacky
sometimes, and I said to myself, 'Della, what's the harm
of letting a nice girl stay a few—?' " The easy rumbling
monologue came to an abrupt halt. Della drew on her
cigarette. "What's it to you, Hank?"

"I'm working for Miss Thayer, and I—"

The door had opened.

Madeira Thayer said pleasantly, "I'm sorry to inter-
rupt, but I thought I heard Mr. Hyer mention my name."

Hyer stood up. For once, Henry Hyer was at a loss
for comment with which to garnish the occasion. Under
the cool appraising glance of the girl in the doorway,
he colored.

Madeira came into the room. She leaned on the back

of a chair and looked at Hyer with edged amusement. Cordero stood in the doorway, his red beard parted in a smile.

"Really, Mr. Hyer"—Madeira studied the embarrassed detective as if he were a clinical specimen as yet untagged—"I thought we had come to another agreement."

Della Doudy, twisting in her chair to stare at Madeira, turned to see the rich flush on Hyer's normally bland face. Her neat mouth opened in amazement. She murmured, "My God." Then to Madeira she said with gusto, "Darling, Fifty-second Street's full of people who've tried to stuff this jack-in-a-box under his lid." She gazed at Hyer again, marveling, turned back to Madeira. "But you're the first ever succeeded."

"Keep out of this, Della," Hyer snapped. He glared at her. Then he looked uneasily at Madeira. "Why, after you and Señor Cordero left my house, Miss Thayer—" He cleared his throat. "Why, you see Angelica was so disappointed, I had to promise her I'd see you again."

Madeira smiled. "So you *have* decided to work for me? How nice." She laughed, easily, her dark eyes warm with enjoyment of the moment. "Sit down, Mr. Hyer." It was a crisp command, like the touch of a whiplash expertly snapped.

Henry Hyer sat down.

Della Doudy blinked.

"As a matter of fact, Madeira," Cordero said, "I thought we were going out with Mr. Hyer."

"We are," Madeira said, smiling. "Get up, Mr. Hyer."

Hyer colored again. "Even a good joke wears out,"
he muttered, but he rose.

Madeira pushed herself back from the chair on which
she had been leaning. She stood straight, small trimly
groomed head high, dark eyes quiet again, her mouth
serious. She said: "Quite. Stupid of me. Will you for-
give us, Miss Doudy, if we take Mr. Hyer away? I'd
no idea you were friends."

"*That's* clear enough," Hyer murmured, and had the
satisfaction of seeing Madeira turn away and walk
swiftly to the door.

As they drove away from in front of the frustrated
fortress, Hyer said testily, "Now you two have had
your little play—"

"So we can all be simple and unaffected with each
other," Madeira broke in. "Being housed up seems to
have left me unusually dull. I still don't understand why
you're here, Mr. Hyer."

"Not that you aren't grateful, of course."

Madeira said, "Um, that remains to be seen. How do
you happen to know everyone whom Pedro and I are
unlucky enough to mention, Mr. Hyer?"

"I've known Della for years. She used to run the
finest house on Park Avenue. I've had business dealings
with the District Attorney of Norcross County." Hyer,
whose good humor was rapidly mending, grinned at the
girl who sat deep in the seat between him and the broad-
shouldered Cordero. Slowly Madeira grinned back.

She said, "Some day, Mr. Hyer, you must tell us all

about yourself. Now what do you want Pedro and me to tell you?"

They returned in thirty minutes. It had been a session of polite feints and parries. Hyer—still nettled enough to resent sharing the information he had gleaned from Klim—had asked only superficial questions. Madeira had added nothing to the outline which Cordero had already given Hyer.

As they approached the theater, Madeira said, "But why should Molloy and Miss Doudy both have—? That is, why did Molloy deny knowing anything about me? And why," she asked, puzzled, "did Miss Doudy pretend she didn't know Molloy?"

"Did Molloy tell you to come to her house?"

"Yes." Madeira stared at Hyer. The tip of her tongue showed for an instant between her lips. "Odd, isn't it?"

"You put the least strain on language of any girl I ever talked to," Hyer observed.

Madeira straightened up between the two men as Cordero turned into the side street. She said quickly, "Pedro, don't stop in front of the house."

"But why?"

"I don't know. I'll feel better if your car isn't— Drive on down the block—there under the trees," she commanded.

A man could, Hyer decided with a stirring of excitement, become accustomed once more to that easy tone of command, the ironically tilted lips, amused dark eyes. . . . He shook his head, thought of something else.

Della Doudy opened the door to them. Hyer noted

that this time she did not turn on the veranda light. The hallway too seemed duskier than it had earlier.

"Have a nice ride?" Della growled. "Beautiful night for it, what with the moon and all."

Hyer, whose nerves were waiting for just such a clue, caught a quick suppressèd nervousness in her manner.

The four of them walked back to the auctionlike living room together. For a few minutes they sat making small and unimportant conversation. Hyer was electrically aware of tension in the room. He waited.

Presently Madeira said: "I must go look at my hair. I feel blown."

Hyer and Cordero rose. At the door Madeira looked back. Her alert glance rested a moment on Hyer. Then she went out.

Hyer, least melodramatic of mortals, could not discard the feeling that something was happening about him, some prelude approaching the main action. There were too many secrets.

While Madeira was gone, the three pretended to keep up the play of conversation which her going had interrupted. But this was a disjointed failure. Hyer caught Della Doudy staring at the hallway door—which Madeira had closed—listening, her lips parted. Cordero was inclined to smile absently as Hyer addressed him and then ask with a start, "I'm sorry, what were you saying?"

Hyer felt himself in the position of a juggler thrust on a darkened stage to replace a performer whose bus-

ily whirling knives and crockery were in mid-career—
and invisible.

The door opened and Madeira returned.

There was an almost palpable silence, which Hyer
tried vainly to analyze.

Madeira was pale. She stood an instant, her hand on
the knob of the closed door behind her. She said quietly,
"Mr. Hyer."

Hyer and Cordero were on their feet. Della Doudy
twisted in her chair, grasping the arms tightly.

Madeira shook her head. "I want to talk to Mr. Hyer
alone, Pedro." She walked across the room, waited for
Hyer to join her at an inner door.

"Where are you going?" Della Doudy demanded.
Her throaty voice broke into near-falsetto.

"I want to ask Mr. Hyer something. Will you excuse
us?" Without waiting, Madeira went through a door
at the back of the room.

Hyer followed her. He and the girl were in darkness.
He felt Madeira's hand on his arm. It was quite steady,
its pressure light but insistent.

"As I started to leave my room, I saw a man standing outside—at the open window," Madeira said softly.
"I pretended not to have noticed. Come. We can surprise him."

Her hand closed on Hyer's. She drew him after her
through a shadowy dining room into which moon-
beams slanted. They crossed a kitchen. Madeira soundlessly unlocked the back door, slipped through.

They went down a shallow flight of steps, stood in the shadow of a massive lilac bush.

It was Hyer's turn to grasp the girl's arm. "Wait a minute," he murmured. "How do you know this man is—?"

"Come."

They moved forward through the wedge of deep dark cast by the silent ugly house. They could hear passers-by streaming from the theater, where a performance had apparently just come to an end.

"There," Madeira whispered as they cleared the jagged stone corner of the house. "The two windows at the end are mine. He was standing at the nearer one."

A light had come on over an alley exit from the theater, dimly illuminating the side of the house. There was no one in sight. Pedestrians hurried by on the sidewalk a hundred feet away.

A clock struck twelve.

Madeira ran on, reached the window twenty feet ahead of Hyer. When he joined her, she was staring at the window.

Its sill was breast-high on Hyer. A cement walk ran directly below it.

The window was closed.

Hyer felt Madeira's hand close hard on his arm. "It's shut!" she whispered in amazement. "When I was in the room it was open—enough for him to have climbed in."

She hurried back the way they had come.

Hyer, turning to follow, stepped off the cement walk.

His foot turned on something solid in the grass. He bent and picked up what he had stepped on. It was a revolver. The grip, which his shoe sole had ground into the dirt, was still warm from a hand.

Hyer dropped the revolver into his pocket as if the faint warmth seared his fingers.

He caught up with Madeira at the corner of the house. Neither spoke as they hastened up the steps and into the kitchen. The girl ran lightly across the kitchen, Hyer following. He collided with the heavy dining-room table and swore.

Madeira had opened the door to the living room. She ran through. When Hyer reached it, he saw her standing midway to the door to the front hall.

Pedro Cordero stood in the hall doorway.

Della Doudy was nowhere to be seen.

Cordero said, "Oh, there you are."

It seemed to Hyer that the observation came languid and laggard after an interminable pause.

Hyer pushed past Madeira and Cordero, walked swiftly along the hall to the massive double doors.

Madeira was at his shoulder as he opened the door.

The room was in deep darkness, the opposite window silhouetted against the glow of the theater exit light.

Hyer's finger found the switch.

Madeira made a sound in her throat.

On the floor, crumpled grotesquely in the bare light of an ornate chandelier, was the body of a man.

5

HYER strode across the room, swept the heavy drapes shut over one window, leaped to the other, and drew the drapes there. Both windows were closed, he noted. Both were locked.

There was a third window, that of the rounded bay which overlooked the street, but here the drapes were already tightly drawn.

Madeira had come a step into the room. Cordero stood in the doorway. Turning from the window he had just shielded, Hyer faced them across the motionless figure on the floor. His nostrils quivered.

Of the three, Madeira was the first to move. She ap-

proached the dead man, hesitated, then knelt swiftly.
Hyer's glance leaped up and to the red-bearded man in
the doorway. Cordero's black eyes, impenetrable, brilliant in that moment, told nothing.

As Hyer knelt beside her, Madeira said softly, "Then
this was the man who—the man who—" She avoided
Hyer's eyes, rose as he bent closer to see the man's
face.

It was the face Klim had described. A deep puckered
scar made a scarlet furrow square across the right cheek.
The tension of this, even in death, drew the corner of
the voiceless mouth up in a fixed grimace and caused
the right eye to droop at a sharp angle. The throat was
bruised and there was a dark welt on one temple.

Like Klim, the man on the floor showed the effects
of his three weeks of exposure and starvation. He was
emaciated, pale, the pallor giving added startling emphasis to the ghastly scar and the bruises. He lay on his
side, hunched forward on the left shoulder, head lolling
at an odd loose angle, left arm crumpled under him,
right arm outthrust.

Hyer looked up. Madeira was staring at him fixedly.
Cordero had come to stand beside the girl. His arm
was about her. Once again, as in that first moment in
Bank Street, Hyer was struck by a subtle quality of
contrast between the two.

Against Cordero's solid, broad-shouldered bulk Madeira was slight, and yet as she stood there, erect, head
high, taut, there was something unassailably command-

ing about her. She seemed unaware of Cordero's arm.
In a moment the big man removed it.

"He was standing at the window," Madeira said
evenly as Hyer rose. "The window was open."

"Stay here, both of you," Hyer ordered. He started
for the door.

"What are you—?"

"Stay here!" Hyer snapped. At the door he whirled.
"And don't touch anything!"

Della Doudy was coming from the kitchen as Hyer
entered the living room from the hallway. At sight of
Hyer's face, she stopped. The bracelets clinked and
were silent.

Hyer caught her wrist and drew her on with him
into the darkened dining room. He closed the door. He
would have preferred in that moment to talk to her
where he could have watched her eyes, but absolute
privacy was more urgent.

He sat on the corner of the dining-room table in the
dark, caught the stocky little woman by the shoulders,
held her against him, his lips touching one dainty scented
ear. This gave him almost as nice an advantage in gaug-
ing her reaction as would sight of her face.

"There is," Hyer whispered, "a dead man on the
floor in Miss Thayer's room." (A tremor, nothing
more.) "Where was Cordero?"

"I don't know, Hank."

"Where were *you?*"

Another tremor. "Looking for you and Madeira,
Hank. Hank, I swear to God I—"

"Before you call Decker Molloy and—"

"Before I—*what?*" She had started violently.

"Listen to me," Hyer commanded. "Miss Thayer is a client of mine. She's going to get a break. I think Molloy will help, but—I *know* you will, Della."

"Hank, I swear I don't know what you're talking about."

"How much would it take," Hyer asked quietly, "for you to forget you ever saw Madeira Thayer?"

"Hank, we can't do that!" in consternation.

"How much?" Hyer asked grimly.

"Hank! Are you crazy?"

"*How—much?*"

She moved in his tightly clasping arms. She said, "I've got a mortgage—"

"How much?"

"The mortgage? Why, five thousand—"

"You'll have five thousand dollars," Hyer said, "if you do exactly as I tell you to—beginning now."

She did not speak for a moment.

"Listen to me," Hyer whispered slowly and distinctly, his lips against her tiny ear. "I never turned a client in to the police without a fight in my life. I'm not going to now. Miss Thayer is going to leave here. So far as you're concerned, she was never near the house."

"But Deck will—" Della stopped in confusion.

"Decker Molloy will be glad to help, unless I miss my guess." He waited. "Where were *you?* . . . Where was *I?*" He pressed her to him, whispered, "Della, my sweet, have you ever sat through a trial for murder?"

She shivered so violently that the emerald clip crushed
Hyer's lip against his teeth.

"Have you got any man's things in the house?" Hyer
asked. "Think!" He shook her. When she moved her
head in a dazed negative, he said, "You've had roomers
before. When roomers don't pay up, you keep their
things."

"No, Hank. Honest to God— Wait!" she gasped.
"Yes, there was a young chap—two years ago. . . .
Trunk in the attic." . . .

"Good. Now you're going to do exactly as I say."

"For five—"

"For five thousand."

She shuddered. "All right, Hank," she whispered.

Madeira and Cordero were waiting in the bedroom.
Cordero was staring down at the dead man. Madeira
stood where Hyer had left her. She was whiter now.
An all but intolerable strain showed in the set of her
lips.

Della Doudy clutched Hyer's arm at sight of the
dead man.

"There is," Hyer said rapidly to Madeira, ignoring
the others, "one chance in five hundred for each of us.
If you multiply five hundred by itself four times, that's
the chance we'll *all* come through. We're going to
move you out of here and— Wait a minute," he said
harshly. "What about servants, hired girl, maid?"

"I fired 'em Saturday morning," Della Doudy whispered.

"Then nobody knows you were here?" Hyer demanded of Madeira.

"No one—except—" She took a step toward Hyer, her eyes wide with sudden terror, her lower lip caught between her teeth. She said something inarticulate and her hands flew to her face as her shoulders shook uncontrollably.

"Madeira," Cordero said. The big man's voice was unsteady.

But Hyer reached the girl before Cordero. He motioned Cordero aside and led her stumbling out of the room, his arm about her convulsive shoulders. His mouth was tight, and the muscles at his temples worked as he led her down the shadowed hall and through the door at the end. He closed the door behind them, lowered Madeira to a chair. He took her wrists gently and drew her hands down.

She did not resist. She lifted her face, ash-white, her dark eyes still terrified, her mouth quivering. "But he—" she began brokenly. "The man in there, he—" Again her face contorted, and she closed her eyes. "He was the one at the window," she whispered.

"Wait a minute," Hyer said quietly. His hands tightened on her wrists. "Hold your breath and count twenty. Funny," he continued in a low casual tone, "funny how much good it does to hold your breath and concentrate on counting. Cure hiccups that way, put out a fire, remember phone numbers—"

"Nineteen," she said, "twenty." She sat up straight, withdrew one hand from Hyer's grasp, touched her cheeks, and drew a long unsteady breath. Gratitude warmed her eyes. "You'll . . . do," she whispered. "Don't go away . . . just yet. Don't leave me with Pedro," she pleaded. She touched the hand still clasping her wrist.

"I'm not going to," Hyer promised. "Now listen to me. When we get through here, I want you to go straight to my house in Greenwich Village. Jonah will fix a room for you. Can you do that alone?"

"Yes." She looked at him steadily, confidence returning.

"You'll have to let Pedro take you to a station where you can get a train for the city. We'll tell him you're going to the St. Julian. Then you can drop out of sight at my place."

"Drop out of—?" She shook her head. "Thanks," she said spiritedly, "I'm not having any more of that."

"Only for a day or two," Hyer said easily. "Until we've had time to look around a little. You're sure that nobody but Doudy and Molloy know you're here?"

"As sure as I can be."

"We'll have to take that chance." Hyer looked at her closely. "What else were you going to say about that chap on the floor?"

"He was the one at the window."

"I know. There was something else."

She looked away. The wrist he held jerked. Madeira made a sound in her throat. "He—deserved it," she whispered passionately. "He—killed—my—father."

When they returned to the bedroom, Hyer said to

Della Doudy, "You and Miss Thayer get her things together. Go over this place with a fine comb. Don't miss
a thread—a hair. You come with me, Cordero. How do
we get to the attic, Della?"

"Straight upstairs. Two flights. The attic door's unlocked, Hank. It's a black trunk. Do you want me to
go with—?"

"You'll be more useful here. Pack Miss Thayer's bags.
Hustle!"

As he ran up the stairs ahead of Cordero, Hyer muttered to himself. He swung about the newel post at the
end of the long straight flight, walked rapidly down a
hall—and stopped.

His nostrils worked. He stood an instant, sniffing,
and then went into a room whose door stood ajar. Again
he stood, sniffing the cigarette-tinged air. He turned on
the light. The room was a bedroom, stiffly and fussily
furnished. The coverlets on the twin beds were of
mauve quilted silk, identical save for a single detail.
While one was decorously plumped and smoothed, the
expanse of the other was marred by a wrinkled depres-
sion.

A table between the two beds bore twin ash trays of
mauve glass. One was virginal. In the other was a match
and the stub of a cigarette. Hyer touched the blackened
end of the cigarette. The glass around it was warm.
The match was a wide flat paper one, torn from an advertising packet. It bore the contour of half a dancing
girl.

Cordero had come into the room and was watching

him. The man's black eyes were intent. When he spoke,
his white teeth failed to flash from the red beard as was
their wont.

"You've had some experience doing this kind of thing,
haven't you, Hyer?" Cordero asked evenly.

"*This* kind of thing? My God!"

"But you can?"

"Can what?" Hyer asked bitterly.

"Gently, amigo." Cordero's black eyes hardened.
"You can protect Madeira."

For thirty seconds the two men faced each other,
waiting like duelists correctly poised.

At last Hyer murmured, "Then that's—how it is?"
It was less a question than a regretful admission.

"You will require a fee," Cordero continued. "I am
ready to pay any fee you ask."

Hyer studied the other man. He started to speak,
caught himself. His glance slipped to the door. The
muscles in his cheeks corded. Then, as if thrusting a
moment of indecision behind him, Hyer looked again
at Cordero, and now his eyes were cool, ironical. "If I
were to ask—twenty thousand dollars . . ."

Cordero stiffened. "You have never charged a fee
like that in your life."

"I've never had a case like this in my life."

Each waited.

"In the first place," Hyer said softly, "we must consider Miss Doudy's—possible financial interest. That
may only be a beginning. I'll take entire responsibility
for the business end." He watched Cordero. "Well?"

"And if you do not succeed?"

"Then we must have a substitute for Miss Thayer," Hyer said. "There are three of us—so far—as candidates, señor. Miss Doudy, though, happens to be an old friend of mine—one of the best friends money can buy." He paused. "If we eliminate Miss Doudy, that would leave only you and me, señor . . . as candidates." Again he waited. "Do you see the value of an incentive, señor?"

They faced each other, *en garde*. The seconds passed.

Reluctant admiration changed the fixity of Cordero's gaze. "You are persuasive, amigo," he murmured.

"Thank you."

"You will guarantee to—protect Madeira Thayer?"

"This way, or some other way."

Cordero fingered his thick sorrel beard. He drew a long breath. "Then so be it—between us."

The trunk was a small one, steamer-size, but heavy. Cordero waved Hyer out of the way and with one easy motion hoisted it to his massive shoulder. Before following the other man from the attic, Hyer seized a striped cover protecting a chair, swept it lightly over the floor to obscure the dust pattern left by the trunk, and threw it back over the chair.

Della Doudy and Madeira were deftly remaking the bed when Hyer and Cordero returned. The girl's two calfskin bags were already packed.

"A man," Della Doudy panted, smoothing the fresh sheet, "*might* smell like Chanel Number Five, but no use having to explain it. Some cops have sharp noses."

The lock on the trunk gave Hyer but three minutes'

difficulty. He threw back the lid. The belongings within were masculine, unremarkable, quite adequate.

Hyer squatted on his heels beside the open trunk, rapidly ripping out labels with his knife, cutting laundry marks bodily from shirts and pyjamas. Madeira and Cordero took the articles and deployed them about the room and the closet.

Hyer looked up once to see Cordero about to drop a meerschaum pipe into an open bureau drawer. "Wait a minute," he said sharply. But at that instant his attention was deflected. Della Doudy had knelt beside him.

"Hank," she whispered, "Hank, be careful you don't leave anything that might—" She looked at Hyer, lowered her greenish eyes in quick confusion. "He was a nice kid," she whispered. "Even if he did run out on me, he was a nice kid. His name was Robert—his first name. I forget his last. It was two years ago." She touched the sleeve of a white sweater. "He was a nice kid, Hank. I wouldn't want—"

Hyer was the last to leave the room. He closed the double panels carefully behind him. Madeira was pulling on her gloves. Cordero stood by the front door carrying Madeira's bags. Della Doudy clutched the carved balustrade, her metal bracelets tinkling.

"Now, you all know your parts," Hyer said rapidly. "If none of us loses his head, nothing in the world can happen. Don't try to make it hard. Don't think of alibis. Nobody needs an alibi. If things go the way they should, then none of us has ever been near here. If they don't—well, an alibi wouldn't be any good anyway. Della will stay here—"

"And meet the police," Della broke in. The bracelets jangled as she shivered.

Hyer said grimly, "You've talked your way out of tighter spots. As for the chap that rented this room, you'll say he was a good-looking youngster with blarney, and when he came to your door this morning you fell for—"

"Never mind, Hank."

"You were lonesome. You don't ordinarily take in roomers, but this youngster—"

"Skip it," Della commanded gruffly. She flushed.

"Your roomer," Hyer continued, "went out this afternoon after he'd unpacked his trunk. You heard him come in about eight tonight. You didn't know he had anybody with him. You didn't hear him go out again. But tomorrow morning, you find a stranger in there dead. If you play it straight, nothing can happen."

"Nothing can—*happen!*" Della gasped. She shuddered. "All night—by myself."

"Rather spend the rest of your life that way?" Hyer asked, unfeeling.

"Suppose somebody sees you people leave?"

Hyer said, "We'll know later. All right. Allez-oop." His tone was light, but his bloodshot eyes were troubled as he looked at Madeira.

Madeira put out her hand to the other woman. "Good night, Della. We're not really running out, you know. If you need us—"

"I know, I know," Della grumbled. She clung to Hyer's arm. "Come here, Hank." Leading him, Della walked down the hall out of earshot of the other two. "You'll be—around, Hank?"

"Within whistling," Hyer promised.

"I'm afraid, Hank," she confessed. "Oh, not for little Della. For her. She's a sweet kid, Hank. That's why I'm doing this. For her. I don't give a damn about the money."

"We've got a bargain."

"But even without the money, Hank. . . . I like her, see?"

Hyer said, "That's good."

Her greenish eyes narrowed. She said, "Oh."

"Never mind, Della."

Her dainty mouth pursed. "Red wants her too, Hank."

"Good night, Della."

But she held him. "Be careful of Mr. Red, Hank," she whispered. "Something tells me he could be bad medicine. You'll watch him, Hank?"

"I'll watch him."

They encountered no one as they walked swiftly to Cordero's car, parked farther along the dark street.

Hyer could feel Madeira trembling as they started. Cordero did not turn on his lights until he had rounded the first corner.

"How can we do an insane thing like this?" Madeira burst out, sitting up rigidly. "Wait, Pedro—wait! We've got to go back. We can't leave Della there—"

"Stop it!" Hyer commanded. He caught the girl's

twitching chin and turned her face to him. "Do you
need a drink?"

"No." She controlled herself. "But we can't—"

"Turn here," Hyer said to Cordero.

"Where are you going?" Madeira demanded.

"To Decker Molloy's."

"But why?"

"If you've told me the truth," Hyer said rapidly,
"Molloy is going to find himself in a dilemma. If Molloy was keeping you out of his brother Reed's way,
then that meant he was trying to prevent a scandal. If
Reed's as disfigured as he looked to be, then he may
not be identified—even Molloy may not tell who he is,
to avoid scandal.

"The chances are that Della will break down in a
little while and telephone Molloy. If she does, I want
to be with Molloy. I want to see what he does—see what
happens afterward. My guess is that Della will take
credit herself for getting you out of the way. She's
strong enough to handle the trunk. She'll tell Molloy
she did it to protect *him*. If it all works out that way—"
He shrugged.

"And if it doesn't," Madeira asked presently, "what
then?"

No one spoke.

Cordero drew up in front of the apartment house
where he had let Hyer out two hours before. The big
man leaned over, shook hands with Hyer.

"Now you two know what to do," Hyer said.

Cordero nodded. "Quite."

"Yes," Madeira answered steadily. "I know."

"We go to the Bronxville station so Madeira can take the one thirty-two to the city," Cordero said. "She will go to the St. Julian. I will go home."

"And tomorrow," Hyer said easily, "we'll compare notes." He gripped the girl's hand. "No mistakes now."

She said, "No mistakes."

Hyer watched them drive away. He started to put his hat on, found his forehead slick, and absently rubbed the back of his hand over it. He muttered, "Of all the—" He blinked, shook his head savagely.

Then he looked up. Counting, he identified the windows of the Molloy apartment. Three were lighted.

He walked briskly into the lobby.

6

THE night doorman, coat off and mop in hand, telephoned sullenly to announce Hyer, then took him aloft.

Again, as on Hyer's earlier visit that night, Decker Molloy himself opened the door. He was, Hyer noted with interest, fully dressed this time. Instead of the Paisley robe, Molloy wore a tweed vest and jacket and gray trousers. This combination, of course, could have meant either haste or nonchalance.

He said, "Hello, Hyer." There was no excess warmth in the greeting.

"I was going by again," Hyer said pleasantly. "I saw your light and decided to drop in for the drink we talked about."

"Oh. Yes. Why, of course. Come in. Always glad to
see an old friend."

(*And always the politician*, Hyer thought. Nothing
in nature but, on occasion, had its uses.)

As he lay back in a comfortable chair and watched
his host at a cellaret, Hyer tried to read hints of nervousness in the District Attorney's manner. This, without
liberal credit to imagination, was a failure.

But when Molloy sat opposite him and raised a highball glass, Hyer saw a burning curiosity break through
the other man's control for an instant.

"Pretty busy tonight, aren't you?" Molloy asked.
The magnificent black eyebrows tilted as he smiled.

Hyer said, "I'm having my troubles."

Molloy put his glass down. He took his hand away,
held it suspended a moment, and then picked up the
glass again, studying it as he swished the liquid. "Troubles?" he asked casually.

"This girl. This Madeira Thayer—"

"Oh, yes, the one you were trying to find. For an
estate, was it?" Molloy looked up from the glass. "Much
money involved, Hyer? Or rather," he added, smiling,
"I suppose a good deal *is* involved or Henry Hyer
wouldn't be—"

"Only twenty thousand dollars."

Molloy put the glass down. It made a thud on the
table.

"It isn't the money so much, though," Hyer continued piously. "I've my reputation to consider."

Molloy pursed his lips. The white scar bent. "I'm

sorry I can't help you out. Tell me some more about it," he suggested.

"The thing's pretty hush-hush," Hyer confessed. "There are some people who'd rather not show in it."

"Oh."

"In fact," Hyer added modestly, "I'm not sure even I know the whole story."

A telephone rang. Decker Molloy rose so quickly that he upset the glass beside him. He strode to a door, said over his shoulder, "Excuse me a minute, old man," and went out, closing the door.

Whisky ran in a little stream from table to rug. Hyer did not move. Lines of strain stiffened at the corners of his rigid mouth. He did not breathe.

When he heard Molloy returning, he lay back in his chair and patted a yawn. But he had never been more electrically awake.

Molloy was now controlling himself with difficulty. The bushy eyebrows were black tufts against his pallor. His lips were compressed, the scar all but invisible. He let himself down into his chair like a man stunned.

"You know," Hyer said through another yawn, "the funniest thing happened to me yesterday. I ran into Jake Felts on the street—you remember Jake Felts, used to handle the legal end for half the show business in New York—a producer didn't dare go into court if Jake was on the other side, but at that I always thought Jake was about ninety per cent—well, anyway I ran into Jake coming out of the Criminal Courts Building, and at first I didn't recognize him."

Hyer went on, inventing an elaborate and pointless anecdote, interlarding it with parentheses, drifting off now into this bypath now that, taking up and dropping random biographies, meandering, garrulous, genial. It was a magnificent filibuster.

Decker Molloy sat opposite him, gray-faced, attentive, his dazed eyes under the shaggy brows never leaving Hyer's face—immobile, untouched by boredom, unresponsive.

Twenty minutes passed. Thirty. Hyer talked on. There was a huskiness in his monotonous voice now. A clock struck two. Hyer continued to talk. Two-thirty. Molloy had not changed his position.

Hyer felt the sharp quiet outlines of the scene begin to blur. The man across from him grew indistinct, unsubstantial. Hyer fought off the hypnotic effect of Molloy's fixed, blindly staring eyes. Still he continued to talk, quietly, endlessly.

Again the telephone rang.

Molloy sighed. It was as if some inner support slowly gave way. The lines of his face sagged. He got to his feet, stood swaying. Hyer, alert again, was shocked by the suffering that showed nakedly in the man's eyes.

"Excuse me again, old man," Molloy murmured. He went to the door like a man carrying a heavy burden.

Hyer waited. He was uneasy. Something had happened which he had not foreseen. He had been ready— but not for this. He had been ready to meet and parry suspicion, girded for an encounter more hazardous than any he had ever undertaken. But now it was Molloy who had been thrown on the defensive, not he. Hyer knew a moment of drunken unbelief.

Then through the fog of his bewilderment a thread-like suspicion began to form. At first this was so tenuous and spidery that Hyer was afraid to consider it. Yet if it should be—

He was on his feet when Molloy reappeared. The District Attorney had recovered somewhat. There was color in his face now. He said, "I'm sorry, Hyer. I've been called out." He spoke quietly, avoiding Hyer's eyes.

"Anything serious?" Hyer asked, interested. He picked up his hat and coat.

"Why, yes. Pretty serious, I guess. Lieutenant Cassius just called me. They've— Excuse me a minute. I'll be right with you. Mind ringing for the elevator, old man?"

Molloy crossed the room to another door, hesitated, opened it, and went through.

He rejoined Hyer as the elevator arrived. The men rode down without speaking. As they went out of the building, Molloy was mumbling. "Wanted to make sure Mother was all right. . . . Maid's out tonight. . . . Hate to leave her when—" He caught himself. "They've found a man murdered, Hyer."

Hyer said, "Well, well. Mind if I go along?"

"No." Molloy touched his arm and indicated that they were to go around the building to the garages at the back. "As a matter of fact," he added, slowly, reluctantly, "I was— I was going to ask you to, Hyer."

An hour later, Hyer waited in the predawn hush in front of the ugly fortresslike house. He leaned on the door of a white-topped police car and watched the square stone pile with its grotesque tower. The veranda light was on. Lights shone on all three floors. Hyer twirled his hat and talked over his shoulder to a policeman in the car.

"Funny," the policeman said idly, "Della Doudy taking on like that. Always heard you couldn't scratch her with a diamond."

"She's got a soft heart," Hyer said absently.

"Yeah? May be. I knew a babe in Rochester like— Yeah?"

Hyer turned, met the squinted gaze of the officer. "What's the matter?"

"So maybe Della's got a soft heart. But why you suppose a stranger with a broken neck upsets her? And how come that broken neck?"

Hyer said, "He was mugged—but good." His attention wandered. A car had turned out of the avenue and was approaching. Its lights flashed up brightly an instant and then were dimmed. The car had been slowing as if about to stop at the curb. Now it swung by them in a swift arc and sped on. But Hyer, whirling to watch it, had time to note the illuminated license number, a short one: XX-2.

"Who carries ex-ex plates, Joe?" Hyer asked.

"Search me, Hank."

Three men came out of the house, stopped to talk on the veranda. Then two of them went back into the house and the third came on toward the street. It was Decker Molloy.

"Ready, Hyer?" he asked wearily.

Hyer said, "So long, Joe." He followed Molloy past two more police cars to the District Attorney's coupé. Molloy opened the door and walked around to get in on the other side.

Hyer waited for the other to speak.

They rode two blocks in silence.

"What do you make of it, Hyer?" Molloy asked in a low voice.

"Murder," Hyer said. "Not much more. Somebody did a pretty clean job."

Molloy was silent a long time. Then he asked with an effort, "You used to know Miss Doudy, didn't you?"

"Quite a while ago, yes." Hyer tapped a cigarette on his case, held the case open to Molloy.

Molloy hesitated, then took a cigarette. He drew a packet of matches from his pocket.

Hyer, noticing a car at the curb ahead of them, leaned forward. But as the license number grew distinct in their approaching headlights, he sank bank. Absently he took the matches Molloy handed him, lighted Molloy's cigarette and then his own.

In the glow of the match, the District Attorney's face was drawn and haggard. After they had parted at the station, Hyer could still see Molloy's strained expression like a haunting after-image.

He had but five minutes to wait in the silent, damp dark. Then a train coasted in and Hyer got aboard.

He settled himself in the smoking car, to think—and to attend to his abused nerves.

He had lighted a cigarette and was about to flick the match into the aisle when his poised thumb stiffened. He murmured, "Ho—ly—"

Carefully, like a man performing a ritual, he laid the burnt match on the windowsill and put his hand into his pocket. Holding his breath, he drew out the packet from which the match had come—the packet he had absent-mindedly forgotten to return to Decker Molloy in the car. He raised the flap of the match packet slowly.

Printed across the row of wide flat matches was a scene representing a stage on which two chorus girls were dancing. Hyer, his eyes bright, took a folded paper from his vest pocket, stared at the single burnt match he had salvaged from the ash tray in Della Doudy's bedroom—the match on which was printed the outline of half a dancing girl. He laid this in place in the packet, fitted the half-outline to its mate.

Closing the flap, he studied the advertising matter on it: "Little Paris—Pittsburgh's Hottest Spot."

"Ticket," the conductor said for the third time.

Hyer took out a bill.

"My niece," the conductor observed, making change, "she collects those things." He pointed at the match packet. "Couldn't spare that one, could you?"

"If it's all the same to you," Hyer answered thoughtfully, "would you take my left eye instead?"

7

DAWN was gray in Bank Street when Hyer let himself in at his door. Wearily he mounted the stairs and entered the long second-floor room where, the night before, he and Jonah had awaited the return of Angelica. Yawning, he dropped his hat and coat on the couch. Then, slowly, he took from his pocket the revolver he had picked up outside Madeira's locked window.

He looked at it with troubled eyes. It was a .32-caliber weapon with a nickel barrel and a black grip. Dirt still stained it where his heel had ground it into the soil. He broke it, looked into the chambers. They

71

were empty. He switched on the bronze lamp, leaned across the red-leather desk top, and squinted through the barrel at the light. The gun had obviously not been fired in a long time. Hyer frowned.

Then he straightened up and shrugged. He made a note of the serial number, unlocked the desk, and took out a dustcloth. He wrapped the gun in the cloth, put it at the back of the bottom drawer, and locked the desk again.

Loosening his tie, he walked back past the grand piano and the doll's house to the garden windows at the rear. Here he yawned again and stood at one open window unbuttoning his vest.

A robin chirped at him from a budding bough of the ailanthus tree in his back yard. The small, privet-bounded squares of lawn and flagstone looked washed and clean. The Burke tomcat from next door lay like a black panther on the roof of Angelica's playhouse and stared yellowly up at the robin on the ailanthus bough.

Across the way an alarm clock shrilled. The alarm was choked off abruptly. A tall girl wearing cerise pyjama bottoms stood for a moment at an open window. She lifted her arms, stretched, stared curiously at Hyer, stretched again, and turned away.

From the street came a banging and clatter as ash-men moved cheerfully from house to house on their early morning round. The panther's tail twitched.

Hyer opened a door at his right and entered a small bedroom. He hung his coat and vest over a chair, and walked through a compact windowless dressing room to a tiled cell beyond.

Presently, showered and shaved, he crawled into bed, murmured, "All's well that ends," and closed his eyes.

There was a tap at the door.

Hyer grinned. He said softly, "All right. I wondered what was keeping you."

Angelica, barefoot and shivering with excitement in her blue bathrobe, trotted in to sit on the edge of Hyer's bed. "I think you never come, Tío Hank," she whispered. "The Señorita Thayer—"

"You said you liked her, honey. So I wrapped her up and sent her home for you. Now run along and let me oversleep." He patted her cheek, curved his hand around the nape of her small neck under the glossy black hair. "Mustn't say anything about the Señorita Thayer being here, though."

Angelica nodded. "But, *tío mío*—" she began, and stopped. She frowned. "Why does she weep?"

"Does she, infant? How do you know?"

"I hear. By her door." Angelica's small mouth drew tight in scorn. "I was ashamed for her. Weeping is for cowards."

Hyer's hand slipped to the little girl's shoulder. "The Señorita Thayer," he said gently, "is no coward, Angelica."

Angelica looked puzzled. "Oh. Then she is—*cómo se dice*—sad?"

Hyer nodded. "She is sad, honey."

"But to weep because one is sad—" Angelica pursed her lips. "Often I, too, am sad, Tío Hank."

Hyer drew her down until her small forehead rested against his own. "What would you say, baby, if you and I went to see your brother in Montevideo?"

She drew back, her black eyes wide and incredulous. "*Por avion?*"

Hyer nodded. "We'll buy our own plane."

"But you said," Angelica gasped. "Montevideo—you said would be too—*cómo se dice*—ex-pen-sive."

"Not any more, honey." Then Hyer's eyes were suddenly wary. "But keep your fingers crossed a day or two. Now run along and quit bothering me."

She bent forward, kissed him, and scampered out.

Hyer awoke to find Jonah bending over him. With one hand Jonah was jostling Hyer's shoulder; in the other he held a telephone with a dangling wire. "A woman, boss. This the third time she called. You talk to her," Jonah commanded testily, "so's I can get Angelica's breakfast." He grumbled, creased his fat middle, bent to plug in the cord, and thrust the phone into Hyer's hand.

"What time did Miss Thayer get here?" Hyer asked.

"Two-thirty. We runnin' a hotel again?"

"What did you do with her?"

Jonah made a lavish gesture and bowed. "She was assigned th' green room, y' Majesty, in honor on account of—"

"Is she up yet? What time is it?"

"Eight o'clock and no—reverse order. Want her to have breakfast up here with you?"

Hyer nodded. "After Angelica gets off to school."

Jonah stopped in the door and looked back. "By the way, boss, that scrawny fellow was here with Mist' Braun—fellow called me 'boy' "—in disgust—"well, he—"

"Klim."

"He dropped in 'bout eight last night. Said he had something else to tell you. Said he'd come back this morning."

"Good."

After Jonah had left, Hyer stared at the telephone in his hand. His eyes were alert, speculative. He murmured, "She loves me, she loves me not. . . . Well." Like a man nerved for a plunge, he lifted the instrument, said, "Hello! . . . Oh, hello, Della."

He listened, propped rigidly on his elbow at first, then relaxing, sinking back to the pillow, the quick alert light in his eyes giving way to relief. "How do you know she didn't get to the St. Julian, Della? . . . Oh, Cordero told you?" Hyer squinted at the ceiling. "Pretty careless of him to call your— You called *him!* Why? Wait a minute," he said sharply. "Where are you now? . . . Well," he grumbled, "even pay stations have ears. . . .

"Oh, she'll turn up. . . . All right, all right, you're worried about her. That won't help any. What about yourself? . . . That's good. . . ." Hyer's face stiffened. "They—identified him? How? . . . Oh, fingerprints. Who is he? . . . *Mallory?*" Hyer drew a breath and relaxed again. As he listened, the last trace of strain left his face. "Robbed a hospital? In Charleston? My, my, you're a mine of information this April morning, aren't you? . . . Well, take it easy, chum. It's all over now but the banking. . . . Forget it. Madeira's all right. . . . I will. . . . I will. . . . Of course I will," testily. "Isn't she a client of mine? . . . Good. Call me up about noon."

He rolled over to put the telephone down, leaned on his elbow, and stared happily out at the sun-filled gardens. Then the merest shadow of apprehension showed for a moment. "Mallory," he murmured. "Robbed a hospital in Charleston."

It was a link no stronger yet than a filament. But the disquieting part was the speed with which the link had been forged. Hyer wondered whether to another man this swift product of the law's foundry might be even more alarming. Decker Molloy, even at a tragic cost, had not identified the dead man for the police. So Molloy had something to conceal. As long as Molloy could continue to conceal it, Madeira had little to fear. But if the harried Prosecutor were pressed too hard . . .

Hyer swung his feet to the floor. Perhaps it was yet too early to relax.

A little after ten, Hyer and Madeira Thayer sat down to breakfast at a table which Jonah had arranged at one of the garden windows. Sunlight slanted in upon the white tablecloth, winked from the cutlery, and burnished the silver domes covering toast and scrambled eggs.

Hyer regarded the girl closely. Her dark eyes had shadows beneath them, but their spirit was untouched. Swift irony still lurked at the corners of her mouth, and when she said, "Tell me what happened," it was a command—quiet, without offense, but uncompromising.

"Decker Molloy never heard of you."

The spirit in her eyes quickened into anger. She said, "Isn't that odd?"

"No. It isn't odd." Hyer took the cover from the eggs. "And it may be pretty convenient. Jonah puts basil in the eggs. Hope you like it."

"I do." She drew a server carefully through the midline of the tumbled eggs, held out her hand for Hyer's plate. "Why convenient?"

When, after a moment, she looked up and caught his eyes on her, Hyer said easily, "We'll skip that one."

She nodded. "It was a stupid question. But I still think it's odd, his—"

"You know who your unlucky caller was last night, don't you?"

Madeira took the cover from the toast. "No. Yes," she added quickly, "I do. I can guess. I guessed last night."

"I was going to remind you of that."

"Reed Molloy?"

"How do you know he killed your father?"

"This man Braun told me," she answered at once. Remembering, she let her eyes grow bitter. Her hand clenched.

"And you believed him?"

"Shouldn't I have believed him?"

"He was lying to you."

"He said Dad had been hurt in the explosion—"

"That's true."

"He said Reed Molloy had pushed my father from the raft—that there had been a witness." Horror and grief showed in her eyes for an instant and her hand trembled.

"Part of that's true. There was a witness. There wasn't any murder. Your father died."

She went white. Her fork halted in mid-air.

"Do you know," Hyer asked, "exactly why Reed wanted to find you?"

She shook her head. She said, scarcely audibly, "I only know why *I* wanted to find *him*."

"He was going to kill you when he found you!"

She hesitated. "How do you know that?"

"You never saw Reed before last night?"

She shook her head.

"He," Hyer said, "had apparently seen you somewhere. Was it your picture your father carried in his watch?"

Grief touched her eyes again, but when she answered, her voice was level and controlled. "Yes, it was my picture. Why?"

"Taken when you were—?"

"I was fifteen. It was in Bogotá." She frowned. "But what—?"

"You lived around with your father in all sorts of places? For instance, Cordero says you grew up at one of his mines."

She smiled. "Estrella Grande, yes." Then she was
sober again, her eyes questioning.

"How long?" Hyer asked.

"We went there when I was seven. We left when I
was fifteen. That was eight years ago. Next question?"

"Things happen around a mine," Hyer observed.
"Anything ever happen to you?"

"Everything," Madeira said promptly. "Snake bites,
malaria, a mule kicked me down a flume, they flew me
out to Caracas with a split appendix when I was four-
teen. I was a walking target for calamity."

"For instance," Hyer said, "were you ever in any
kind of scrape that might have left somebody with a
grudge?"

Her eyebrows lifted. "Possibly. I wasn't a model ado-
lescent. Latin tempers live long."

"This would be a *norte-americano* temper."

"You mean Reed Molloy?" she asked, astonished.

"I mean Reed Molloy. When he saw your picture in
your father's watch, he announced he was going to
kill you. He might have been out of his head on the
raft. But what happened last night," Hyer added
grimly, "gives point to the story. It was a fifteen-year-
old's picture in the watch. He recognized it. About the
time you were fifteen, something must have happened
to— Yes?" he asked, noting the change in her expression.

Madeira shook her head. "It would be too fantastic
a coincidence—his being with Dad on the raft, I mean,

and being the same man . . ." She looked thoughtfully out the window. "I once shot a man."

"You get more interesting all the time."

"It was at Estrella Grande," Madeira continued slowly. "That's in the Caroni country, south of the Orinoco."

"Cordero's mine?"

"Yes. Gold. Every once in a while diamonds turn up at a working like that. One August there was a run of them. Little ones, nothing exciting, but a steady flow of good industrial stones. Before we could ship them out, more than a hundred and fifty carats had piled up in the company safe.

"The safe was in the office. The office was part of the superintendent's house. One night I was staying with the superintendent's children when I heard a noise in the office. I went in to see what it was. The light wouldn't work, but I heard a sound at the safe and then heard a man running to the window. He turned a flashlight on me and fired. I fired back.

"He missed. I didn't. But he got away—and so did the diamonds. There was a trail of blood running down to the river. Later on—after I'd come North to school that winter—we heard that a badly wounded man had been taken care of by some Indians for several months and had paid his way in diamonds." Madeira stopped. Her mouth twisted.

"What else?" Hyer asked.

"The man had been wounded in the face. The Indians said he was horribly disfigured when he could travel again." She stared at Hyer, shook her head slowly. "Do you see what I mean by a coincidence?"

"Maybe. Maybe not. In most professions there's a kind of larceny fringe of sharpshooters. They prowl around the edges of the trade and do odd jobs. Say Reed Molloy was one of these. There's pretty good evidence he was shadowing your father for somebody on the boat. If he undertook errands like that, then swiping diamonds might have been right in his line. After all, when you come right down to it, how big a fraternity does the whole mining business make? You were always running into the same experts, weren't you?"

Madeira nodded. She traced circles on the tablecloth. "Then you think Reed Molloy may be the man I shot nine years ago, that he recognized my picture in Dad's watch, and when Dad told him where to find me—" She stopped abruptly. Her eyes widened.

Hyer nodded. "Exactly. Which brings us to the Honorable Decker Molloy, Norcross County Prosecutor. It's beginning to shape up. Let's take a hypothetical case. Solid Citizen with political ambitions loses track of Younger Brother in South America. Suddenly Younger Brother turns up, nervous and gun-shy. He's robbed a hospital.

"Then let's say a girl appears and asks questions about Younger Brother. Solid Citizen scents some kind of a scandal and is polite and cagey.

"Then Younger Brother lets the cat out of the bag. Say he gets drunk and brags about what he's going to

do to a girl who damaged him pretty badly one time.
He shows older brother a picture of the girl. Older
brother looks at the picture in the back of a watch,
snaps the case shut—"

"And Decker Molloy," Madeira said rapidly, "knew
that the only way to prevent a really serious scandal
was to keep me out of Reed's path."

"Not the only way," Hyer corrected. "There was
another—a pretty drastic one. But maybe it wasn't feas-
ible just then."

Madeira's mouth stiffened.

"Decker Molloy," Hyer said, "was in Della's house
last night while we were. He lighted a cigarette with a
match from a Pittsburgh night club. He was in Pittsburgh last Wednesday and Thursday. I checked this
morning."

"He was there—last night?"

"Yes. And later on—though it tore him apart inside—
he didn't show by a flicker that he'd ever seen the dead
man before."

"His—*brother*," Madeira whispered.

"So you see," Hyer said slowly, "as long as Molloy
is still on our side, he's a very useful citizen. He's not
likely to ask questions about you, because that would
raise some embarrassing questions about himself, and
about his long-lost brother Reed, and about—" Hyer
turned his hand over. "Once a thing like that gets
started unraveling, nobody knows where it will stop.
And Decker Molloy wants to be Governor some day.

"But right now," Hyer continued, "Molloy is a little

unpredictable. For a while, awake or asleep, twenty-four hours out of every day, he'll be seeing his brother there on the floor—seeing himself standing above his brother and turning away without a word. For a minute last night I thought he'd not quite bring it off . . ." Again Hyer turned his hand. "He did. But he's hurt. How badly, there's no way of telling—yet. The trouble is that for a little while it'll get worse. Until he gets over it, he'll be—unpredictable."

Madeira stared down at the gardens drowsing in the sun. On a flagged terrace, a baby and a dachshund wrestled while a young man in a pointed beard worked at a diminutive flower bed. The Burke tomcat leaped over a privet hedge and glided forward on his belly toward a robin that was listening for worms at the corner of Angelica's playhouse.

"But I wonder," Madeira said slowly, "whether what we did—to the room, I mean—was necessary."

"It didn't hurt." Hyer's reply was that of the modest craftsman touched in his pride.

Madeira frowned and shook her head. "Using an innocent man's things to—"

"You saw what I *did*," Hyer said with some asperity. "There isn't a chance he can be traced."

"But can you be sure you didn't leave *some* clue that the police—"

"Police?" Hyer's tone was that of simple astonishment. "When *I* did it?"

Madeira smiled. "You're very sure of yourself, aren't you?" She stared at Hyer, laughed. "Pedro once re-

marked that modesty and merit have only one thing
in common."

"What?"

"The initial letter." She laughed again. "At that, I
think I like you, Henry Hyer. I've always liked extro-
verts."

Before the warm amusement in her eyes, Hyer looked
away. "I may not be sure of myself," he grumbled,
"but I'm always sure of the police. You can bank on
them to—"

"Boss," Jonah called, putting his head around the
hall door at the front of the room. "Man downstairs
to see you. Klim, you said his name was. Called me 'boy'
last night," Jonah snorted. "What'll I do with 'im?"

"I'll come down." Hyer rose from the table. "Will
you excuse me, Miss Thayer?"

"Certainly. What do you want me to do this morning?"

"Stay put," Hyer said hastily, "till they post the first-
quarter score anyway. Don't even let Cordero—"

"I won't."

Hyer, remembering, leaned on the back of his chair.
"By the way, last night you didn't want to be left alone
with Cordero."

Madeira looked out the window. "Never mind."

Hyer started to ask a question, shrugged. "If you
stay on the second floor here and the third, you'll be
all right."

"I'm sure I shall." When Hyer had almost reached

the door, she called, "Wait." There was the quick whip-flick of authority in the command.

Hyer turned.

"If they should trace the chap whose trunk you used," Madeira said evenly, "then one of two things must happen. Either you see that he is cleared immediately—in your own way—or I shall do it myself, by telling exactly what happened."

"It's a bargain," Hyer promised.

A bargain lightly enough made. But at the moment Hyer's attention was on Eben Klim, waiting below to see him.

8

EBEN KLIM had been neat and shipshape the night before. But this morning he showed the effects of a buffeting by some all too mortal storm. His pale eyes were bleary and red-ringed, his cheeks and bony chin untidily stubbled. His hand-me-down suit, which had been brushed and presentable when Hyer last saw him, was now wrinkled and dusty. A stain was splashed down the front of the jacket.

Hyer said, "Well, well, do you think it was worth it?"

Klim looked abashed. "I musta had a drop too much, Mr. Hyer."

Hyer surveyed the damaged engineer. "Maybe you were better off on that raft. I hear you stopped in again last night."

Klim's Adam's apple cavorted. He took an unsteady step toward Hyer. "That's why I come back this morning," he said huskily. "That's why I come back last night. I think I know where the watch is, Mr. Hyer. You said you'd pay—"

"Where?"

"I don't know exactly, but—" He caught Hyer's sleeve with a palsied hand. "I know where *Reed* is, anyway," he whispered.

"Good. Let's go see him."

"If he's got the watch—"

"Suppose we wait and see," Hyer suggested.

As they rode south in a cab, Klim explained jerkily how he had come by his information.

"I didn't tell you the whole story last night, Mr. Hyer," he confessed. He plucked at his mouth. "You remember I said I'd been watching a place up in Highbridge in case Reed went in or out? Well, I told you he didn't."

Hyer nodded. "I knew you were lying."

Klim's Adam's apple bobbed. "How'd you know?"

"Watching you. So you did see him?"

Klim nodded. Again he touched his mouth with shaking fingers. "Last Saturday morning—very early it was—I see Reed come out. I'd just got there. I followed him. He took a train to New York. I followed him on

the train, and when we got off I pretended to bump
into him by accident and be surprised to see him.

"Well, *he* was surprised, all right. At first I guess he
was kind o' suspicious of me, but that didn't last—considering what we been through together. Anyway we
had a drink or two and finally he said he'd had a fight
with his family and did I know a cheap place he could
stay for a day or two until he finished some business
he'd started. So I took him down to this hotel we're
going to and we both got rooms."

"And then you ran right around and told Braun you'd
found Reed?" Hyer asked ironically.

Klim was embarrassed. "Well, no, sir, I didn't right
away. I wanted to know a little more about what I
was doing first, and since I knew where Reed was—"

"By the way," Hyer asked curiously, "what gave
Braun the idea you could do this kind of a job anyway?
It takes experience to pick a man up and shadow him."

"I had plenty of experience of that sort," Klim answered proudly. "I used to do investigating on the harbor police in Frisco. I had plenty of experience on the
harbor police. Put more'n one organizer outta business
in my time. I can take care o' myself—in any way you
wantta name, Hyer. That sort of thing comes back to
you."

"Then maybe you can give me some help some time,"
Hyer said, interested.

Klim's bony jowls reddened under their gray stubble.

They stopped in front of a shabby hotel frequented
by anonymous male transients not yet reduced to the

marginal economy of the Bowery. Klim led the way up
the steps. In a barren lobby, under the flat inevitable
musk of stale tobacco and disinfectant, four lodgers
lounged. The clerk, a heavily padded man in a vest and
green arm garters, glared at Klim.

Klim straightened his shoulders. He said: "Now I
don't want no 'more of that talk. I had all I'll take, hear?"
His voice rose shrilly. "You'd no call insulting me, way
you did."

"Insulting you," the padded one echoed scornfully.
"Insulting *you?* After the racket you. made all night,
wonder I don't throw you out on your can right now."

Klim marched stiffly up the stairs, mumbling. As he
and Hyer went down a dusty hall, he said, "I guess I
did kick up some, at that. Got a little too high maybe."
He scowled. "But there's no call for him to—" He
touched Hyer's arm, said in a low voice, his pale eyes
alight: "That's his room right there—that fourth door.
Reed's, I mean. Hasn't been out of it since we checked
in Saturday afternoon." He moistened his lips. "You
thought what you're going to tell him, Mr. Hyer?"

Hyer said, "Let's see if he's friendly." He rapped on
the door.

Klim breathed noisily. A man came from another
room, looked at them incuriously, and plodded downstairs.

"Maybe he went out after all," Klim whispered.
"Knock again."

Still no response. Klim put out his hand nervously and
turned the knob. The room was locked. He shook the

knob, stepped close, and called, "Reed!" guardedly. "Reed, it's Klim. It's all right, Reed. Open the door." He looked at Hyer, alarmed. "Don't suppose anything's happened to him, do you?"

Hyer said, "We can see." He took out his key case, opened it. Among the keys was a slender steel shaft, hooked sharply at the end. Hyer slipped the hook into the keyhole, maneuvered it a moment, and turned it. The bolt clicked. Hyer opened the door.

Within was a square untidy chamber furnished with a white iron bedstead, a straight chair, and a cheap bureau. In one corner was an ancient clothes press, its warped doors hanging ajar. The dusty window, giving on an air shaft, was shut.

Klim seized Hyer's arm. "Look!"

On the bureau lay a gold watch.

A moment later they left the room. Hyer locked the door, and Klim hurriedly led the way to the stairs and up another flight. Midway down the hall, he stopped, took out a skeleton key, unlocked a door, motioning Hyer through.

This room was similar, as far as furnishings went, to the one on the floor below. But whereas that had been merely untidy, here the disarrangement showed the touch of a connoisseur. The green shade at the window had been jerked from its roller and lay in a crushed heap on the floor. Against the wall to the right stood the iron bedstead, and directly in front of them as they entered, two feet to the left of the head of the bed, was a small square washstand in lieu of the bureau.

The washstand bore four empty whisky bottles and a cracked glass. The bed was in astonishing disarray: not only were the bedclothes rumpled, but there were three longitudinal slits in the mattress toward the bottom, and the iron frame itself had suffered damage to the extent of three bent rods at the foot. From the state of these, one might have assumed that a light tractor had been hitched to them to draw the bed forward, and that after a tussle the bed had won.

On the floor between the washstand and the head of the bed were whisky splashes. The unaired room was richly alcoholic.

Hyer said, "It's a wonder they don't throw you out."

"We needn't stay here," Klim said apologetically. "It's only I thought it'd be better to come up here to my room to look at— That's it!" eagerly, as Hyer took the watch from his pocket.

It was a gold watch, perfectly plain except for the initials J. T. in a small wreath engraved on the back. From the ring hung a hasp of gold with a fine gold chain dangling from it.

With his knife Hyer pried gently under the lip of the case. There was a snap and the hinged back opened. Hyer turned it up. At his shoulder Klim breathed hoarsely.

In the tilted watch case was the portrait of a girl. It was a laughing, youthful face. But the spirit in her eyes, the swift decisive line of her lips, the imperious lift of her young head, were all unmistakable.

"Ought we take it, though, like this—without Reed knowing?" Klim asked anxiously.

"It isn't his," Hyer said. He closed the case, applying pressure with his thumbnails at its rim. "Well, I guess you've carried out your part of the bargain, Klim. If I had that much cash with me—"

"I'd take a check. I'd take a check, Mr. Hyer."

Hyer said, "All right." He took out his checkbook and pen, wrote a bearer check for $250, and waved it a moment before handing it to Klim. "They'll cash it for you at the Sheridan Square branch," he told the engineer.

Then Hyer removed half a dozen letters and papers from his inner breast pocket, dropped the watch into one of the envelopes, and put the sheaf back. He said, "Let's go."

When they reached the lobby, Klim was on the point of hurrying past the critical clerk without comment, but Hyer stopped.

"Any idea," Hyer asked easily, "when the chap in Thirty-four went out?"

"On your way, fly cop."

Klim plucked at Hyer's sleeve.

Hyer leaned on the counter affably. "I'm only a businessman, brother." He drew a bill absently through his fingers. "I don't suppose you saw him go out. Scar on his face."

"Um. Maybe I did. Maybe I didn't." The clerk got up from his chair, gave each of the green armbands a hitch, and strolled over to stand before Hyer. "Last night. Six o'clock. Half-past."

"By himself?" Hyer asked, smoothing the bill.

"I guess I wouldn't know that—yet."

Another bill worked its corner free from Hyer's left hand.

The clerk gave a tug at his armbands. "Fellow came for him. Fellow about your size. Had a red face and parted his hair in the middle. Him and Thirty-four went out together. Maybe a little before seven last night. If he's run out on his—"

"Then this will cover it," Hyer broke in, moving the bills across the counter.

The clerk took the money. "Are you kidding?"

Hyer was going out the door with Klim when the clerk called, "Hey, copper!"

Hyer turned.

The clerk beckoned.

Hyer walked back.

"Maybe I could tell you something else, too," the clerk mumbled. "Maybe."

Another bill made its appearance in Hyer's folded hand.

"This guy that took Thirty-four out last night, well, he come back this morning. The guy about your size with the crack in the middle of his hair."

Hyer said, "That's interesting."

"We caught him sneaking out Thirty-four's room. Got in with a skeleton key, I guess. We threw him the hell out. About two hours ago."

Klim was waiting for Hyer on the sidewalk. "What did he want?" Klim asked quickly.

"Braun came back this morning. He got into Reed's room. They threw him out."

"How'd Braun find out Reed was here, do you suppose, Mr. Hyer?"

"That's the sixty-four-dollar question," Hyer said. "Don't rush things. Well, I'll be seeing you."

They shook hands.

"If I can ever do anything else for you, Mr. Hyer—"

"You never can tell. Drop in any time."

Two minutes after leaving Klim, Hyer stopped in at a delicatessen, called his bank from a wall phone, and stopped payment on the check he had given Klim. He promised to confirm this with a note, and dispatched the note by messenger.

From the delicatessen he took a cab to police headquarters in Center Street and visited for a time with his good friend Schultz, of the fingerprint detail.

In response to Schultz's wizardry, two well-defined thumbprints presently showed on the smooth gold back of the watch. The obliging Schultz photographed these for Hyer.

They discussed the prospects of the Dodgers, and then, inevitably, talked of Angelica.

"Still have trouble with her playing hooky from school?" Schultz asked.

"Do you know," Hyer said, brightening, "the youngster's developed an interest in natural history."

Schultz expressed admiration. "I used to collect Croton bugs myself when I was a kid in the Bronx. More'n once I like to scare my sister into fits with a box of 'm. Usually little girls don't take to Croton bugs. So Angelica—"

"Who said anything about Croton bugs?"

"Well, you tell me Angelica—"

"Natural history," Hyer said testily. "Museum trips, dinosaurs, birds—crocodiles."

"She's a bright one, all right, Hank. You ought to bring her in again soon. The boys up in the telegraph bureau were talking about Angelica other day. They're fixing something for her birthday."

Hyer beamed. "We'll drop in tomorrow."

"Tomorrow's a school day," Schultz said, disapproving. "Anyway, Hank, I'm going up to the country tonight, and I wouldn't want to miss Angelica."

When the negative Schultz had made was dry, Hyer wrote a memorandum, folded the negative into it, and sealed them in an envelope. He asked Schultz to initial and date the envelope and lock it in his desk.

"The chances are," he told the stolid Dutchman, "we'll tear this up in a day or two. But in case I need it, I'd like to know it's in good hands."

"You got a case, Hank?"

"I may have one. By the way, I wonder if one of the boys could check a Smith and Wesson serial for me." He took out the slip on which he had written the number of the revolver he had picked up and later wrapped away in his bottom desk drawer.

Schultz said, "Why, I guess so, Hank. You in a hurry for it?"

"No. But there's one thing I'd like now."

"Yeah. What's that, Hank?"

"Do you suppose you could pin a tag on those prints you found on the watch?"

Schultz looked at him sharply. "Well . . . I suppose for my own curiosity I could, Hank. Then— Well, if you happened to look over my shoulder—" He shrugged. He studied the print he had made from the negative, jotted down a notation, and started off to his files.

"Mind if I use your phone, Schultz?"

"Maybe," Schultz said, "you'd like me to clean out my desk so you can feel at home. Or we could ask the Commissioner to step out for a little while. Sure, go ahead, Hank."

Hyer called Jonah, asked guardedly about Madeira. Perfectly comfortable, Jonah reported. He added that Señor Cordero had called twice, and that the District Attorney of Norcross County had asked Hyer to telephone him before noon.

Hyer pursed his lips and leaned back to stare thoughtfully at the ceiling.

Schultz came back. "What is this, Hank? A gag?"

Hyer tilted forward. "Not that I know of. Why?"

"Them prints—you don't know who made 'em?"

"Haven't the foggiest idea. Friend of mine found the watch."

Schultz regarded him closely. "According to the rec-

ord, Hank, they belong to a guy which I got no business giving you his name."

Hyer looked interested. "You don't say."

"Hank," Schultz said sternly, "if you're going in for
blackmail—" He grinned. "Me, I had a run-in with this
guy a while back, too. He's too big for his britches.
Wouldn't exactly make me mad to see him whittled
down a little bit." Schultz sat down. "Name's Decker
Molloy. He's D.A. up in Norcross County. That's whose
prints are on your watch, Hank."

9

NORMALLY Henry Hyer was not a man who allowed
the whim of a District Attorney to disturb him.

Toward District Attorneys—toward all officials who
owe their salaries to posturing before the polls—Hyer
had always maintained the skeptical attitude of the professional man. A message from a police sergeant, a sum-
mons from a lieutenant of detectives—these Hyer was
wont to treat with the respectful attention due one
working man from another.

But District Attorneys, in addition to being politi-
cians, were lawyers, a breed for which Hyer had at
best a tepid toleration.

Thus the fact that Decker Molloy wanted him to telephone Highbridge would not, under usual circumstances, have been sufficient to deflect Henry Hyer from the busy completion of his appointed rounds.

This forenoon, however, was an exceptional case. When he left police headquarters, he took a taxi at once, gave his address in Bank Street, countermanded this within two blocks, told the driver to take him to Grand Central Station, and changed his mind again three minutes later.

"The Exporters Trust Company," he said. Then, as he became aware of his own indecision, alarm awoke within him.

He stifled the alarm with characteristic briskness, and made himself consider the situation coolly.

A man had been killed—a man whom he had never heard of until the evening before, and in whom even now he had only the most acutely negative interest. Acute enough, indeed, to bring a dew of perspiration to his temples as he examined it.

The dead man had been the brother of an ambitious Prosecutor, who, the night before, at a rather tragic cost to himself, had concealed this accident of genetics from the police. Save for the fact that this made him a psychological hazard, Molloy's reticence had appeared at the time to be most fortunate.

But now a disturbing number of loose ends were showing—and too many people were threatening to have nuisance value.

Braun, for example. If Braun had left the hotel with

Reed, then it was conceivable that Braun had taken Reed
to Highbridge. The episode was not difficult to imagine:
Braun insisting on Reed's surrender of the watch, Reed
demanding a favor in exchange—a lift to Highbridge,
after which Braun could bring him back to town and
get the watch.

Hyer's neck prickled. It was even conceivable that
Braun knew of Madeira's presence in the Highbridge
house—that, having failed to secure the watch and being
somewhat less than amiably disposed toward Hyer,
Braun might liquidate his own nuisance value by telling
what he knew about Madeira.

In retrospect, the hasty camouflage of Della Doudy's
front room loomed like a pursuing thunderhead, curling
forward, threatening to break over him.

Why, Hyer asked himself furiously, had he plunged
into that foolish deception like an amateur, without first
making sure of his ground? But even as he asked the
question, he saw Madeira Thayer's white face as he had
seen it the night before—and the acid of his self-contempt was neutralized by an odd long-dormant feeling.

The vice-president in charge of personnel at the Exporters Trust Company received him briskly. "Mr.
Hyer? Oh, yes. What is it?"

At another time, Hyer might have been flattered by
the hint that his name was not unfamiliar. Just now he
was anesthetized to flattery. *Mr. Hyer? Oh, yes . . .*
Oh, yes, what? Hyer asked himself grimly.

"A Miss Madeira Thayer in your South American
div—"

"Miss Thayer left us very suddenly last week, Mr. Hyer."

It was as if he had touched a spring, coiled for precisely this cue. An instinctive and faultless warning sounded within Hyer.

"Could you tell me where—?"

"I'm sorry, Mr. Hyer. Miss Thayer simply left us."

A minute later, Hyer emerged from the vice-president's office, walked halfway across the anteroom, stopped, felt in his coat pockets, felt in one trousers pocket, the other trousers pocket. Under the curious gaze of two secretaries he made an anxious search of his immediate wardrobe, murmured audibly, "I must have left it," turned and walked swiftly into the inner office again.

The vice-president, holding a telephone to his ear, looked startled and made a move to rise. Reddening, he hastily covered the mouthpiece: "Yes, yes, what is it now?"

Hyer lifted an eyebrow. "If I'd timed it a little better," he confessed, "I might know." He added amicably, "It was worth trying anyway," and went out again.

But when he entered his cab, his amusement had vanished. He had been expected at the Exporters Trust Company. They had been waiting for him, waiting for him to come and ask just the question he had asked. At the moment, Hyer's feeling was chiefly one of resentment that he had so easily fallen into a trap. Not a serious trap, to be sure—so far. But a man in the open can afford to stumble only so many times and no more.

Hyer thought again of the watch in his pocket, of the sealed envelope in Schultz's desk at police headquarters. The fingerprints in that envelope had abruptly taken on a new and sharply satisfying significance. That maneuver at least had the odor of sanity about it. If worst came to worst, he—and Madeira—might both find it useful to have assumed a certain trenchant nuisance value themselves. If worst came to worst . . .

Hyer grasped the strap, sat back in a corner of the cab, and stared narrowly out at Broadway as they sped toward Bank Street. His abstraction lasted until they turned into the final block. Then it broke with a shock. Hyer sat up. The inner warning was like a struck bell.

In front of his house was a car. There was something familiar about the car. Any one of a hundred others might have roused this same feeling of recognition quite harmlessly—but no other would have borne the license number XX-2.

The reverberant alarm lasted only an instant. With its passing, and even before he knew who his visitor was, Hyer experienced a swift and refreshing sense of release. However sound his cautious defensive tactics might have been, an infallible instinct told him that from now on Madeira's only defense against these ominously converging accidents would be a bold offensive.

He must stake everything on attack. He must seize the initiative while he could, gamble on blocking this steady infiltration of puzzles before Madeira's position was hopelessly confused.

In short, he must without delay begin to provide a

live decoy toward whom these accidents could be deflected before they assembled too cozily about Madeira Thayer.

"Something tells me," Hyer murmured as he ran up the steps, "that things are about to happen." He sounded extraordinarily cheerful, like an impatient craftsman from whose plans some cramping restriction has suddenly been lifted.

Oddly, he did not think of the $20,000.

Jonah Hastie opened the door as though he had been lying in wait. "Got an isitorvay, boss," Jonah muttered, stubbing his thumb toward a closed door. "Couldn't get rid of 'im."

"What about . . . ?" Hyer pointed upstairs.

"Fine, boss. Been a little bit restless maybe, since you went away."

"Restless?" Hyer let Jonah help him off with his coat, walked toward the door.

"You know, walkin' up and down. Made a phone call," Jonah added.

Hyer turned, frowning. "Phone call? Where?"

"Exporters Trust Company. Asked if she had any mail there. Rice boiled over just then, so I didn' hear anything else she—"

"Hello, Hyer." Albert Braun had opened the door.

Hyer's expression was at once bland and unrevealing as he turned to Braun. He said, "Well, well, this *is* a coincidence."

"I thought you might be surpri—" Braun's squarish

florid face stiffened. "What do you mean, a coincidence?"

Hyer walked into the small sitting room where Braun
had been waiting. He opened his cigarette case, held it
out.

Braun ignored the offer. "What do you mean, coincidence?" He smoothed his sharply parted hair.

Hyer leaned against the low mantelpiece and looked
at his visitor curiously. "What have *you* been doing?"

Braun flushed. "What do you mean?"

"Why have the police got a pickup order for a car
with your plates?" Hyer asked.

"That's absurd," Braun snapped.

"That's what I thought. If I were you, I'd drop in
at some precinct station and raise cain."

Braun's eyes narrowed. "Do you mean you saw a
police order to—to stop my car?"

"Somebody must have read a license wrong," Hyer
said. He waved his hand. "It happened out of the city
anyway. Well, what can I do for you this morning, Mr.
Braun?"

Braun took out a cigarette, tapped it nervously on the
back of his hand. "Where out of town?"

Hyer shrugged. "Jersey, maybe. It seems this car
they're looking for was mixed-up in a killing. I didn't
pay any attention—didn't know it was yours until I saw
your number just now. Well," hospitably, "sit down. I
thought you'd written me off."

"It couldn't have been my car," Braun said, blustering.

"Mine wasn't out of the garage all night." He frowned. "That is, so far as I know."

"Forget it," Hyer said easily. "Maybe I got the number wrong anyway."

Braun shook his head in annoyance, sat down.

Hyer, now thoroughly enjoying himself, said, "Have you got some more advice for me this morning, Mr. Braun?"

Braun looked uncomfortable. "I hope you don't hold that against me. As a matter of fact," he went on frankly, "I owe you an explanation. I don't know what got into me last night, Hyer. I came to you then for the same reason—well, the same reason Miss Thayer did."

"You wanted the watch?"

The directness of the question caught Braun off guard. "Why—why, yes. As a matter of fact, I did."

"Did? That means you don't any more? Why?" Hyer looked at the other man with new interest.

"It's a complicated story," Braun said hastily. "I suppose Miss Thayer and Cordero said they wanted you to help find a certain Reed Molloy? Yes? Well, you see, Hyer, this Reed Molloy was working for—some people I'm working for." Braun watched Hyer's eyes. "He was with Miss Thayer's father. It was his business—Reed Molloy's, that is—to see that nothing happened to John Thayer. But the boat they were on was wrecked and they had to take to a raft. Klim—the chap with me last night—was also on the raft."

"By the way," Hyer asked, "how did you happen to run into Klim? At an auction?"

"No. I went to Charleston and saw him in a hospital."

"Molloy?"

"No, damn it, Molloy was the man I wanted to find."

"We seem to be getting mixed up," Hyer said mildly. "I thought you wanted to find a watch."

"I did. Molloy had the watch."

"*Had* the watch?"

"Wait a minute. Thayer had given the watch to him just before he died on the raft. Klim told me about it— told me about Thayer's giving his watch to Molloy and asking Molloy to take it to his daughter in New York if—"

"Oh. So you brought Klim back from Charleston to help you find Molloy?"

"The man was destitute. It was common charity to lend him a hand."

"Common charity," Hyer observed, "is another of those virtues I hadn't read in your face. Why is the watch so valuable?"

Braun hesitated. Then with a burst of candor he said, "I might as well tell you the whole thing, Hyer. John Thayer was smuggling diamonds out of the Orinoco country. At the time, I was willing to bet five hundred dollars that his watch was full of diamonds."

"You mean, you were willing to pay Klim five hundred dollars if he found Molloy for you?"

"Exactly."

Hyer said, "My, my," in amazement.

"But," Braun continued, "I've since found I was

wrong. Whatever diamonds poor Thayer had must have gone down with him."

"How do you know?"

"Because I have his watch."

Hyer blinked.

"The watch, of course," Braun went on, "has no worth to me. But I suppose it must have a great sentimental value for Miss Thayer. Since you told me she is a client of yours, I thought perhaps you could tell me where to find her."

Hyer said, "That's too bad. She left for Kalamazoo on the Wolverine last night. But I'll be glad to see she gets the watch."

"On the Wolverine?"

"Maybe it was later. I was never good at train times. But if you'll leave the watch with me— Well, I guess that clears everything up, doesn't it?"

"I'm sure it does," Braun agreed warmly. He took a gold watch from his pocket, looked at it a moment, and handed it to Hyer. A line of salt crystals was white in every groove.

"Mighty good of you to do this," Hyer said gratefully. "I'm sure Miss Thayer will appreciate it—as much as I do."

"It seemed the only reasonable course. Otherwise—"

"Otherwise," Hyer said genially, "I might have made myself a nuisance. Is that it?"

"Not at all, not at all."

"Just the same," Hyer advised, walking to the front door with his caller, "I'd clear up that license-number business if I were you. Since you weren't anywhere near Highbridge—"

"Highbridge?"

"That's the place. I read something about a murder there this morning. Chap named Mallory." Hyer's eyes brightened. "By the way, the paper said he'd been in Charleston not long ago. Seems he'd been in a hospital there and—"

The bell rang. Hyer opened the door.

On the stoop stood Angelica, home from school for luncheon. Her black eyes were bright with excitement as she looked up at Hyer. "Tío Hank," she asked eagerly, "is she still here, the Señorita—"

"No, honey. She finished your dress and went home." Hyer moved, trying to bring Braun into Angelica's view.

She frowned. "My dress? But I mean the *muy simpática*—" Angelica caught sight of Braun. Her small eager face went blank. She said, "But, of course, Tío Hank."

"Run on in, Angelica," Hyer said gently. "Jonah's getting your lunch ready."

Angelica trotted down the hall.

Braun looked at Hyer. His square florid face was thoughtful. His mouth tightened and then tilted in a smile. He murmured, "The—*muy simpática—señorita* . . . ?"

"Little blonde dressmaker," Hyer explained. "Angelica's quite fond of her."

"Oh." Braun made a move to take off his coat. "I believe I'll wait a little."

"Fine," Hyer said with cheerful hospitality. "We'll phone the Sixth Precinct and they can send a man around to clear up this mistake about your license number. Save you a trip."

"Thanks, but I guess I'd better—" Braun's eyes were sardonic. "I'd hate to get you—and the *muy simpática señorita*—mixed up in any unpleasantness."

"Well, just as you say."

"But I may be seeing you again, at that."

"It depends on you," Hyer said easily.

Braun shook his head. "No, Hyer. I think it depends . . . on you."

Hyer grinned. "In that case, *hasta luego*."

10

ANGELICA crept around the newel post from where she had been hiding on the stairs leading to the floor below. Her wiry little body drooped with shame, but her small firm jaw, badge of a rugged Basque ancestry, was obstinate.

Hyer regarded her quizzically.

In a small voice, she said, "I am sorry. I did not see the man, Tío Hank." She stood before him, regretful, stubborn, on the point of tears.

Hyer put his arm about her shoulders and drew her into the small sitting room where he had had his interview with Braun. "It's all right, baby. Only next time you must remember. I told you it was a secret about Señorita Thayer's being here—a secret between you and me and Jonah. Secrets you don't talk about."

"Yes, Tío Hank," Angelica said humbly. Then her black eyes flashed. "But I did not talk—to nobody."

"Anybody," Hyer murmured, looking out as Braun's car moved swiftly away.

"*Nobody!*" Angelica repeated stubbornly. "Not one single body—all morning."

Hyer patted her shoulder. "Good. Let's have lunch."

Angelica held back. "The man who just go now—you call him Braun?"

"Right, baby."

"Albert Braun?"

"Yes. Why, Angelica?"

She puckered her forehead. "Tío Hank, the Señor Cordero who came last night—came with . . . *Tu sabes?*"

Hyer cocked his eyebrow at her. "Yes. What about Cordero?"

"Why have Señor Cordero a letter from Albert Braun, *tío mío?*"

"Why does Cordero have a—" Hyer tilted her chin up. "Angelica," he demanded sternly, "have you been picking pockets on the hall tree again?"

Vigorously Angelica tried to shake her head. "It is *my* fault if a coat it fall down as I pass?" she protested. "And if a letter it fall out when I elevate the coat to—"

"And you read the letter, you little felon?"

"No-no-no-no," hastily.

"That's better." Hyer's tone was one of regret.

"It was sent to Señor Cordero from a Señor Albert Braun in—*cómo se dice*—the town?" Angelica asked innocently.

"Charleston?"

Her black eyes lighted impishly. "Then you are *not* angry, Tío Hank! You wish to know what was in the letter, no?"

Hyer sighed. "All right. I'm responsible for you before the law."

Angelica looked demure. "It was only the cloak of the letter. It said to return to Albert Braun in that town. I did not—"

"At least," Hyer grumbled, "you were honest enough not to read it." He tweaked her ear. "Now get down to lunch or you'll be late to school."

She stopped and looked back as she started to run down to the basement. "Next time, Tío Hank, if you keep him *un minuto* longer before he come for his coat—"

"*Angelica!*"

When Hyer entered the long room on the second floor, Madeira Thayer turned from a garden window and came toward him. She said, "Molloy called you. Does that mean—?"

"Nobody knows what it means, Madeira—except Molloy." It was only when she looked at him oddly that Hyer realized that he had called her Madeira.

"Then you haven't found out anything?" she asked.

"I wouldn't say that. I had a talk with Braun. Braun says your father was smuggling diamonds."

Her dark eyes blazed. "*That's a lie!*"

Hyer nodded. "I thought so."

"My father," she said, her voice shaking with passion, "was the most honest man in the world. If you—"

"All right, all right. I only—"

"Let me finish," she commanded furiously. She took a step toward him, her fists clenched, trembling. "Whom have you repeated that lie to?"

"No one."

Hyer, whose attitude toward veracity was at best a pragmatic one, found himself, for once in his life, oddly respectful toward the truth.

"I hope that's true," Madeira said evenly. "Because, Henry Hyer, if I once hear that you've repeated that lie to a soul—you'll be sorry for the day you were born." She leaned back against the big desk. "What did Braun say?"

She had made no apology for her outburst. She was, Hyer decided, not one who often needed the cover of apology. His admiration for her quickened. He took from his pocket the watch which Braun had given him. "Because Braun had to have some excuse for being interested in this."

Madeira held out her hand. She turned the watch over, looked up at Hyer, puzzled. "This?"

"Braun asked me to give it to you," Hyer explained. "He said it was the watch your father gave to Reed Molloy."

"But it couldn't be," Madeira protested.

"No," Hyer agreed, "it couldn't be. Because," bring-

ing out the other watch, "this is the one your father gave
to Reed."

Madeira seized the gold watch. Grief flooded her eyes,
and she bit her lip. "Yes," she said softly, "this was—
Dad's." She turned away, walked to a chair, her shoulders quivering. But when she sat, facing him, she was
calm. "Where did you find it?" she asked.

Hyer described his trip to the shabby hotel, the dis-
covery of the watch in Reed Molloy's room, the account which the clerk had given of Reed's departure
with Braun and Braun's return to the hotel that morning.

"Then perhaps Braun took him to Highbridge last
night," Madeira said quickly. "But why would Braun
have pretended he found Dad's watch?"

"Because he thought the real one was gone. He's apparently got his own reasons for not wanting Henry
Hyer to be too curious—*about* those reasons."

Madeira considered this. "What would have made
him think the real watch was gone, Henry?"

"We know Reed didn't have it on him after he was
killed." Hyer watched her, watched comprehension
dawn in her eyes.

"But you said Braun had been back to Reed's hotel
room this morning," Madeira said slowly. "If he could
have got into the room, he would have found Dad's
watch—the way you did."

Hyer nodded. "That's the hard part," he agreed.

Again she was thoughtful. "But perhaps the watch
wasn't there when Braun went to the hotel this morn-

ing? Perhaps someone put it on the bureau afterward—before you and Klim went in."

Hyer said, "That's a possibility."

Madeira looked out of the window. "If that should be the case," she said slowly, "then whoever put the watch in the hotel room—may be the one who killed Reed." She turned to him, a flush in her cheeks, her eyes determined. "I can't wait here any longer. It's like being trapped. I've got to be doing something. This man Braun—"

"Has your friend Cordero ever mentioned Braun?" Hyer asked.

"No. Why?"

"Braun went to Charleston to look for Reed. Why would he have written a letter to Cordero from Charleston?"

"But Pedro had never heard of Braun until Friday," Madeira said in amazement.

"Tell me something about him."

"Braun. I don't know—"

"Cordero."

"Oh. Why, Pedro and Dad were great friends. Pedro's a Venezuelan. For generations his family has been one of the wealthiest in South America. Pedro hasn't lived in Venezuela himself since he was fifteen, I think."

"How old is he now?"

"Thirty-five or six. He went to Harvard and then to the Sorbonne, where he studied philosophy—"

"Where he *what?*"

Madeira smiled. "Pedro's a curious person, Henry. He says he can trace his lineage back to the Caribs. Their women were the fabled Amazons, you know. He speaks I don't know how many languages—even Gaelic; his grandmother was Irish. He has composed a piano concerto, and two of his water colors are in the Metropolitan. He is one of the shrewdest businessmen I've ever known. All right, you asked me to tell you about him."

"Why didn't you want to be left alone with him last night?"

"Sometimes," she said frankly, "I'm afraid of him."

"Why last night?"

"I suppose I was upset. Have you heard anything about Miss Doudy?" she asked, as if anxious to turn the conversation. "Do you suppose she—?"

"She's all right. She's worried about you. So is Cordero," Hyer added. "He called Della up this morning when he couldn't find you at the St. Julian."

"Poor Pedro. I feel guilty about deceiving him. Can't I—? All right." Madeira nodded quickly. Then she asked curiously, "Why was I sent to Miss Doudy's house, do you suppose, Henry?"

Hyer chuckled. "From away back, Della's been accustomed to doing favors for District Attorneys—usually on request."

From the speaker below the desk came Jonah's voice. "Boss, you don' want y'all lunches up there, do you?"

Hyer leaned over the desk to touch the switch. "We do. We're ready any time you are."

Pause.

"I guess I didn't hear you," Jonah said doubtfully.

The telephone rang.

"You heard me," Hyer retorted. "I'll take the call." He picked up the telephone, said, "Hello! . . . Oh, hello, Lieutenant."

Madeira sat forward, watching Hyer intently as he talked. When he put the phone down, she rose. "Who was it?"

"Chap named Cassius," Hyer said carelessly. "Well, I hope you have a good appetite. Jonah—"

"You called him Lieutenant? Is he a police lieutenant? He *is*." Madeira drew a quick breath. "What did he want?"

"What did he—? Oh, Cassius. Why, you see he's an old friend of mine. Calls me up every once in a—"

"Boss," Jonah's voice came from the speaker under the desk, "guess that takes a load off your mind, don't it—way they picked him up like that?"

Madeira looked hard at Hyer. She said, "Oh."

"Hear me, boss?" Jonah asked.

Hyer depressed the switch. "I heard you."

"Jonah," Madeira called, "what did Lieutenant Cassius say?"

Jonah said, "Oh, oh." There was a click.

Madeira walked over to confront Hyer. "Tell me!" she commanded.

"Butting into my business," Hyer grumbled.

"Tell me," Madeira repeated. She reached for the telephone. "Or shall I call Lieutenant Cassius myself? He's in Highbridge, isn't he?"

The telephone rang. Madeira's hand was quicker than Hyer's. She said, "Mr. Hyer's residence," crisply. She listened. "Who shall I say is calling, please? . . . Oh, yes, Mr. Molloy. Just a moment." Madeira covered the mouthpiece, said firmly to Hyer, "If you want to talk to Decker Molloy, you're going to hold this so I can hear, too."

Hyer nodded, took the telephone from her as she came to stand at his shoulder. He held the receiver up-tilted so they both could listen, said, "Hello, Molloy."

"I've been trying to get you," the Norcross County Prosecutor said wearily. "I want to have a talk with you, Hyer."

"I'll be in all afternoon."

"Can't you come up here?"

There was a moment's pause. Madeira glanced aside at Hyer, nodded quickly, said with her lips, "You'd better go."

"All right, I'll come up to Highbridge."

"I want to talk to you about that girl you were looking for," Molloy said, lowering his voice.

"What about her?" Hyer asked, interested.

There was another pause. Madeira compressed her lips.

"You know what happened last night—while you were with me, Hyer."

"While I was with you?"

"Hyer, they've arrested the man who rented the room." Molloy's voice shook. "The room we found—the body in."

Madeira said quickly, "Mr. Molloy, that's all a mist—"

She made inarticulate smothered sounds, fought at the hand Hyer clamped over her mouth, kicked at his shins.

"What's that?" Molloy asked, nervously. "Who was that, Hyer?"

"I heard it, too," Hyer said swiftly. "Somebody must be listening in up there." He tightened his grip on the struggling girl. "Go outside and call me back."

Decker Molloy said, "My God!" in consternation and hung up.

Hyer released Madeira, yelped as she landed one well-aimed kick.

Madeira stepped back, her dark eyes furious, her breath coming fast. "Why did you do that?" she gasped.

Hyer bent to rub his damaged kneecap. "If you were Angelica's size, I'd spank you."

"Do you realize what we're doing to an innocent man?" she asked fiercely.

"Do *you* realize," Hyer snapped, "what can happen to *you* if— Anyway," he protested, "you said if this happened, you'd give me a chance to do it *my* way before you—"

"Your way is too slow," the girl said briskly. "Get your coat. I'll be down by the time you're ready. We're going to Highbridge." She ran out and up the stairs.

Hyer stood for three minutes, staring blankly at the door. "Too slow," he murmured. "Too—*slow!*"

From the speaker, Jonah said cheerfully, "Guess you won't want lunch, then, will you, boss?"

Hyer's finger leaped angrily for the switch. "Were you listening outside this door, you—?"

"Nossuh, nossuh, boss. Not me. Angelica."

Footsteps pattered rapidly through the hall below. " 'By, Tío Hank."

"*Angelica!*" Hyer shouted.

The front door slammed.

For a moment, Hyer's expression was that of a man driven perilously close to madness.

The telephone rang. Hyer's nostrils twitched. There was a hunted look in his eyes as he picked up the phone. He said, "Hello! . . . Oh, hello, Molloy. . . . I don't know. I heard it, too. How well do you trust your staff? . . . Well, anyway, maybe I'd better not come to your office. Where can I meet you?" . . .

Madeira hurried down the stairs, appeared in the doorway pulling on her gloves. She saw the phone in Hyer's hand. Her eyes grew stern and she took a step toward him.

Hyer backed away. He said rapidly, "How about Della Doudy's? Quiet again by now, isn't it? . . . Don't act like that," testily. "I'm trying to do you a favor. . . . All right, I'm trying to do myself one, too. If you don't want to help, that's your—" . . . He listened, partially mollified. "Della Doudy's, then. As soon as I can get there—an hour maybe."

"As soon as *we* can get there," Madeira corrected grimly. "Are you ready?"

Hyer sighed. "At least," he muttered, "Grand Central Station will be nice and quiet." Little crow's-feet of anxiety showed at the corners of his eyes as he followed Madeira from the room.

He caught up with her at the front door. "For the

last time, Madeira, will you obey orders and stay here?"

"No!" Then her eyes softened. "No, Tío Hank." She smiled. "We women are a problem, aren't we?" Then, lowering her voice, she said, "Don't think I'm not grateful—for what you're trying to do for me. It's only that— Well, I've never been in the habit of having things done for me. I'm a little awkward at it."

Her hand was on the latch, but she made no move to open the door. Under Hyer's steady gaze, color rose in her cheeks. "You've never had a client like me, have you, Henry?"

"Yes," Hyer said. "Once." He added, the words coming slowly and with a peculiar effort, "I was foolish enough to fall in love with her."

Her color deepened swiftly, but her eyes did not waver. "And she—?"

"She was killed in a train wreck." The muscles at Hyer's temples twitched. "Now do you know why I said no when you and Cordero came here last night?"

Madeira looked away.

"Even then," Hyer said harshly, "you reminded me of her. There are some things I don't want to go through twice." He caught himself, added with brittle irony, "This time I've insured myself—for twenty thousand dollars."

Madeira opened the door.

At the curb Pedro Cordero was stepping out of his car.

11.

CORDERO shouted, "Madeira!" His teeth gleamed white against the thick sorrel beard. In three long strides he was across the sidewalk and up the steps, seizing her, oblivious to Hyer, oblivious to passers-by, his relief at finding her bursting in a torrent of Spanish.

The torrent slackened. Cordero's black eyes rested on Hyer. "But you did not tell me—you did not call me at once when you found her."

"I've been busy," Hyer said drily.

"Madeira . . . Madeirita. Would you," Cordero asked sadly, "have me go mad? Where have you been? Why did—?"

"I've been here, Pedro." Madeira freed herself. "I wanted to call you, but—"

"But our good friend prevented you?" Cordero broke in lightly. The red beard parted in a smile, but his glance as it leaped at Hyer was hostile.

"Not at all," Madeira said calmly. "I wanted some time by myself."

"By yourself? Ah, yes. And how is the small black-eyed one?" Cordero asked Hyer cordially.

"Come," Madeira said. "We'll tell you about it on the way. You can take us."

"Take you?"

"To Highbridge." She was running down the steps.

Cordero, on the point of following, stopped abruptly and turned to Hyer. "Highbridge? This, then, is another one of your ideas?"

"No, hers," Hyer said shortly. "Maybe you can stop her."

"Um. Stop her? Why should I stop her, Hyer?" Cordero's black eyes grew mocking. "You seem to have managed Madeira's affairs up to this point."

"I'm being paid to."

"Yes," Cordero said affably, "you are being—paid to. You will not forget that, amigo?"

"Forget twenty thousand dollars?"

Cordero eyed him closely, nodded. "Good. There must be one small condition, though, Hyer," he added softly. "It had not occurred to me last night that such a condition might be necessary."

"Are you two coming?" Madeira called from the car.

"At once, my dear," Cordero answered. He turned again to Hyer. "You are to remember that your relation to Miss Thayer is solely that of a professional man to—"

"You needn't worry," Hyer said shortly. "Come on."

Cordero touched Hyer's arm when Hyer would have passed. "I do not worry, amigo. When it becomes necessary to worry—I act. It is a quaint habit, what?" The white teeth flashed. "*Pues bien, vamos.*"

Hyer, blandly expressionless, followed Cordero down the steps and was about to get in beside Madeira when he hesitated. A man, approaching them, had broken into a run and was making vigorous gestures of dissent at Hyer.

Hyer grinned at Madeira. He said, "Here comes a business caller. I'll have to talk to him. We won't be long."

Eben Klim came up to him panting. Klim's long stubbled face was a study in frustration and fury. "Say, Hyer, what kind of a bank you—?"

"It's all right," Hyer broke in. He took the engineer by a lank arm and steered him up the steps. "Come in and I'll tell you about it." When they were inside the house, Hyer said, "I stopped payment on the check."

"You stopped— Then it wasn't the bank?"

"Mustn't jump at conclusions, Klim. People start runs that way."

"Then," Klim said with asperity, "I think you owe me a explanation."

"I stopped payment on the check because I didn't want to lose you."

"You didn't want to—lose me?" Klim asked nervously. "What've I done?"

"Nothing as far as I know," Hyer reassured him. "But it occurred to me that if for any reason that watch began to burn my fingers, I'd need somebody to help me explain how I came by it."

Klim said, "Oh, for a witness."

"For a witness. And a handyman. I may need both sooner than I'd expected. How would you like a job?"

Klim looked doubtful. "I'd like my two-fifty first."

"Wouldn't you like to run it up to five, Klim?"

Klim's Adam's apple quivered. "In cash?"

"In cash."

"We—ll—"

Hyer said, "Good. Now in about an hour, I may need you to back me up in my story about the watch. I'll be in a house in Highbridge."

"Highbridge?"

"Where you found Reed, yes."

"You mean the same place I found him?"

"No. This isn't an apartment house. Number thirteen Abbey Street—like a corner of Sing Sing broken off and dropped behind a movie theater."

Klim swallowed. "What's that about Sing Sing?"

"The same architect drew 'em both. Only he was still sane when he did the Big House."

"Don't talk like that," Klim said nervously. "I keep thinkin' how you and me walked into Reed's hotel room and took—"

"All right. Now listen to me. I want you to take the

first train from Grand Central, go to Highbridge, hire a
cab, park where you can keep an eye on Number thirteen Abbey Street—"

"If it's all the same to you, Mr. Hyer, I think
maybe—"

"It's not," Hyer said briskly. "I've a job for you to
do. I want it done. Maybe two jobs," he added. "How
about it? Five hundred dollars for a full day's work."

Cupidity showed in Klim's pale eyes. He touched his
lips with his tongue. Then he shook his head. "No. If
you don't mind, Mr. Hyer, I'll just—"

"You saw the chap with the carrot whiskers out there
in the car," Hyer said genially. "The girl is Miss Thayer.
You followed both of them to my house last night for—"

"Now look," Klim complained, "you said something
like that in the saloon last night. How'd you know I—?"

"Because it was such a smooth piece of work, Klim."

"We—ll . . ."

"And because Braun admitted you'd done it for him."

"Why, the—"

"Wait a minute. What harm was there in it? In fact,"
Hyer said with enthusiasm, "I was so impressed I decided I'd give you a commission myself some day. Well,
I'm offering you one now. For another two hundred
and fifty dollars."

Klim shifted his hat from one hand to the other. He
said, "*Another* two-fifty," meaningfully.

"You've got my check, haven't you?"

"For what good it does." Klim shook his head. "No,
Mr. Hyer, I think I better wait around for Reed. Some-

how I feel kind of responsible for him, seeing it was me took him to that hotel."

"Then you shouldn't have told Braun where to find him," Hyer said calmly.

Klim swallowed. "Did Mr. Braun tell you I told him?"

"How else could he have found Reed?"

Klim looked dejected. "I been calling Mr. Braun all day. I couldn't get him."

"Braun's been pretty busy. All right, will you go to Highbridge for me?"

Klim shook his head. "I'm waiting for Reed to come back."

"Then you'll wait a long time, Klim. Reed's dead."

Klim's Adam's apple dove into his slack collar. "Reed —dead?" he gasped. He clutched Hyer's arm. "How do you know?"

"I saw him."

A new and violent nervousness seized Eben Klim. "But if Reed's dead—then the watch— If it comes out you and me got the watch, Mr. Hyer, the watch he had—"

Hyer nodded. "So you see, do you?"

"Mr. Hyer," Klim said fervently, "I don't want to be mixed up in any more of this. I'll thank you for my—"

"You'll get it, Klim. But for a little while I still need you. Though," Hyer added slowly, "not quite as bad as you—may—need—*me*, Klim."

Klim's gaunt face twitched.

"Together," Hyer said, "we've got a perfect story. Separately—" He watched Klim's struggle, said softly,

"You wouldn't want to have to tell *your* story—and have me forget *my* lines, would you, Klim?"

"Threatenin' me!" Klim said bitterly.

"Not at all. Unless," Hyer added, "you're threatening *me*, Klim."

The engineer's eyes widened. "My God, no, Mr. Hyer!"

"Fine. Then we understand each other. Now you're to go to Highbridge and wait in Abbey Street where you can see Number thirteen. If I need you, I'll signal."

"And if you don't—"

"Wait there. In case Cordero—the one with the red beaver out there with Miss Thayer—comes out, either by himself or with anybody else, you're to follow him."

"Suppose he gets away from me?"

"Accidents will happen. But you strike me as too good a workman for that," Hyer said. "Here. This for the ticket to Highbridge and cab fare at both ends. Keep out of saloons." He gave Klim a bill. "And how far do you think you could get if you tried to run out on me?"

"Run out on five hundred bucks, you mean," Klim said gloomily.

"A man after my own heart."

Klim's eyes narrowed as he put the bill away. "Is that really on the level about the extra two-fifty?"

"For being on hand if I need you. For bird-dogging Cordero if I don't."

"And if it comes out you don't need me or I lose 'im?" Klim asked anxiously.

"Pay anyway. What can you lose?"

Klim scratched his jaw. "Sometimes I wisht I'd told Mr. Braun there in Charleston to take his old ticket to New York and—"

"Where's your sporting blood, Klim?"

"I got none," promptly.

The bell rang. Hyer opened the door. Angelica looked up at him, ducked, and started to run past. Hyer caught her. He said sternly, "Playing hooky again!"

Angelica shook her head vigorously. "I forget my notebook, Tío Hank."

"You'll be late," Hyer grumbled. He patted her, gave her a start to the stairs, looked after her as she ran up.

Klim coughed. "Your daughter, Mr. Hyer?"

Hyer said, "Why—why, *yes.*"

"Looks like a bright one. Takes after you, I guess."

"She can be stubborn," Hyer agreed.

Klim shifted from one foot to the other. His pale eyes were worried. He coughed again. "You say Reed—"

Hyer raised his hand.

Angelica slid swiftly down the banister, launched herself off like a reversed ski-jumper, whirled, and landed facing the men.

"Where's the notebook?" Hyer demanded.

Angelica was demure at once. "I guess at school. I guess I forget—*cómo se dice*—double cross." She looked swiftly at Klim, smiled at Hyer, and went to the door.

"You know what curiosity did for that kitten," Hyer warned.

Angelica laughed and ran out.

Klim moved uneasily. "You say Reed's—really dead?"

Hyer guided him through the doorway. "I'll tell you all about it later."

When Hyer got into the car, Madeira said, "It seems to me I've seen that man before." .

Hyer looked at Cordero quickly. Cordero's attention was on the street before them. He ignored Eben Klim's long loose-jointed figure as they sped by the engineer.

"Maybe you have," Hyer said to Madeira. "He runs a newsstand in Times Square," he continued easily. "Everybody sees him some time or another."

He was watching Cordero, waiting for Cordero to turn his brilliant black eyes. But Cordero was intent on traffic.

"He does some stool-pigeon work on the side now and then," Hyer continued, neatly embroidering his lie.

"You know the most interesting people," Madeira murmured.

"He's the one that helped me find your father's watch," Hyer said, like a matador leaning in with the final stroke.

Cordero gave a start. He looked squarely at Hyer. "Helped you *what?*"

"Pedro," Madeira said excitedly, "we hadn't told you, had we? Henry found the watch."

"*Henry* found—the *watch?*"

But to Hyer's annoyance the moment was lost, for he could not be certain whether it was subject or predicate which gave to Cordero's question its color of suppressed passion.

"My congratulations," Cordero added quickly. "By

God," he said in loud admiration, "you're an amazing man, Hyer. Where is the watch, Madeira?"

"I left it at the house."

"Oh." Cordero's flashing smile became a grin as he looked across Madeira at Hyer. "Then you can send it to us when you go back . . . 'Hen-ry. But," he rushed on in high enthusiasm, "you must tell me how it happened . . . Hen-ry."

"Must I?" Hyer asked coolly.

"I'm curious."

"You are," Hyer snapped.

Then as Madeira's elbow prodded him sharply, the stiffness left Hyer's mouth and the cold brittle light in his eyes changed to a speculative amusement. "Tell him about it . . . Madeira."

12

AS they approached Highbridge, Cordero said thoughtfully, "Of them all, your friend Klim seems best qualified . . . Hen-ry." There was mockery in the last word.

Hyer, catching Madeira's eye, swallowed the retort he was about to make.

"Klim," Cordero continued, musing, "was with Reed and John Thayer on the raft. We do not know exactly what may have happened during that time. Braun told Madeira one story. Klim told you another. But is it not possible that for some reason Klim felt he had a score to settle with Reed?" His eyes lighted. "Over the watch, for example. You said Klim was angry because Reed had slipped away from the hospital with the watch."

"Klim," Hyer agreed, "has another point in his favor."

Madeira was sunk down between the two men, taking no part in the conversation.

"What is that?" Cordero asked, interested at once.

"Klim's the only one of us who doesn't know that Reed was Decker Molloy's brother."

"Of . . . *us?*" Cordero echoed. "That pronoun does not recommend itself. We were talking of those who might be suspected of the murder."

"We were," Hyer said grimly. "We still are."

"Um. Yes. Unpleasant subject. But to recapitulate: Gallantry compels one to mention first Miss Doudy, who—"

"Stop it!" Madeira commanded. "You're like a ghoul, Pedro."

"—who was quite conspicuously absent during the time you and Madeira were examining the outside of the house. And who," Cordero added, the beard curling back from his white teeth, "struck me as quite capable of breaking a man's neck.

"But," he continued thoughtfully, "if in the case of Klim we have a motive without a modus operandi, Miss Doudy confronts us with a marvelous opportunity for action—and no motive.

"*Pues bien.* There is Molloy himself. Let us say he was considerably embarrassed to find his brother the burglar of a hospital. Then imagine his consternation on learning—if your theory is correct, Hyer—that Reed intended to murder Madeira. That would account for Molloy's concern to get Madeira hidden. He would go to any length to prevent a scandal which might ruin his political ambitions—*did* go to a rather tragic length, in fact, when he declined to recognize his brother."

"And how," Hyer asked, "are you going to put Decker Molloy inside the house when Reed was killed?"

Madeira bit her lip.

Cordero looked swiftly at Hyer. "Alas, how? Then we must discard the otherwise promising District Attorney, what?"

"You've two left," Hyer reminded him, "before you get too warm."

"Braun?"

"He's one," Hyer agreed.   —

"And the other?" Cordero asked politely. "Oh." He laughed. "Before I get—too warm. That's good, Hyer. But what would *my* motive have been?"

Madeira struck her gloved fist on her knee. "Will you two stop making a farce of this!" she said angrily. "Think of that poor fellow they've arrested. Think what we've done to him. What will his life be after this? Whispers . . . people whispering about him and looking sly . . . people nudging each other and twisting everything he does into nasty lies. I hate myself for—" She broke off, looked up at Hyer with quick determination. "I want to see him, to talk to him, Henry."

"All right, Madeira. Later."

"Now," she commanded.

"They won't let you."

"If the District Attorney himself tells them to?"

"What makes you think—?"

"I believe," Madeira said slowly, "that the District Attorney will be very glad to do a small favor . . . for me."

Hyer started to speak, tightened his lips disapprovingly.

Cordero was silent.

Presently they stopped in front of the stone house in Abbey Street. Seen in daylight, it was no less ugly than at night, though for an added and startling reason. For the heavy untrimmed blocks which composed its square bulk and squat toothed tower were mottled with red, as though once in its shocking youth the stones of the house had been painted.

The front yard was barren except for a massive lilac bush, its boughs green-tinged in the soft April sun. On the lawn of the house next door a dogwood was in full bloom. The street was quiet. After its night and morning of notoriety the house had, as Hyer had expected, slipped again into sullen dotage.

Madeira started to protest as Cordero turned off the motor.

"You wanted to see the District Attorney," Hyer reminded her. "We've a date with him here." He stepped out, looked along the street for Klim. No cab was in sight.

Madeira slipped out, evading Hyer's hand. She hurried toward the house ahead of the two men.

"Do you think this is exactly wise, Hyer?" Cordero asked as they followed. "Not, of course, that I should be one to question your judgment."

"Decker Molloy," Hyer said shortly, "is suggestible."

"Oh."

"It's not wise, no. But this may be a better place to talk to Molloy than the courthouse." The corner of Hyer's mouth twitched. "There'll always be time for the courthouse later."

Della Doudy opened the door as Hyer and Cordero came up on the square veranda. "Ma-deir-a!" she cried, her bass voice breaking in falsetto. She seized the girl's arms drew Madeira to her convulsively, the carillon of bracelets jangling.

Della held Hyer back as Madeira and Cordero ran the gauntlet of autograph-memoirs to the living room at the end of the hall. "Henry Hyer," she said in a rumbling stage whisper, "if you've got no more sense than to bring that poor girl back here where—"

"Did you ever know me to do a thing without a reason?" Hyer demanded.

Della looked at him hotly. "I never did—before."

Steps sounded on the veranda.

"There can always be a first time," Hyer said grimly. The bell rang.

"What's this," she whispered, "about your asking the District Attorney—?"

"Now, now," Hyer said. "We're away past that chapter. I'll let Decker in." He went to the door. His hand, lifting to the knob, froze. Through the curtained trefoil window in the panel there showed the silhouette of a peaked cap. Over his shoulder, Hyer said rapidly: "And

~when I make a mistake, it's a lulu. Get Madeira and the beard upstairs. Fast."

Della Doudy's reflexes were trained by long years of exacting apprenticeship. She sped soundlessly down the hall and disappeared.

Hyer backed away on the balls of his feet until he came to the ornately carved double door of the room Madeira had occupied. He opened this to give himself the show of having come from the room—and said, "Oof!"

He was face to face with the District Attorney of Norcross County.

Decker Molloy showed the effect of some grueling strain. His eyes, under the heavy black brows, were sunken, sleep-famished, haggard. His face was gray with fatigue. The white scar stood out sharply across the taut set of his mouth.

"You answer the door," Hyer said. "It's official. You and I have been looking over the room. I'll give you cues."

Molloy shook his head. "No."

"Then I'll go," Hyer said softly. "And I'll say you just came back for the match you left in an ash tray up-stairs last—"

Molloy walked past him as the bell rang again.

Hyer waited inside the room, alert, expectant, unper-turbed. He heard Molloy open the door, heard him say, "Hello, Cassius."

Hyer was examining the interior of a deep closet when the two men came into the room. He walked out, dusting his hands, said, "Congratulations, Cassius. I hear you got your man."

The police lieutenant with Molloy was a tall muscular man with the seamed impassive face of a sachem and snow-white hair. He said, "Yes. We did." He had a solid deliberate way of speech, as if whatever he said were likely to become substance of an official report and thus deserved forethought.

"Good police work," Hyer said admiringly. "It looked hard last night. Not even a laundry mark."

Molloy went to stand at a window.

Lieutenant Cassius stared impassively at Hyer. "There was a meerschaum pipe. In that dresser there."

(*In the dresser where Cordero put it*, Hyer thought savagely. The meerschaum pipe had been wrapped in a sock at the bottom of the trunk; Hyer had determined to destroy the meerschaum as too unpredictable an item to leave for the police, had seen Cordero drop it into the drawer—and forgotten.)

"A lot of men smoke meerschaums," Hyer observed, fighting off a self-contempt that was like nausea.

Cassius considered this. "It had been broken, repaired. A new screw piece was in the stem, but the stem was old."

As the enormity of this error opened slowly before him, Hyer felt the thunderhead of disaster curling forward, dropping . . .

Cassius moved his head toward the door. Hyer followed him into the hall. Molloy had not turned from the window. To Hyer's glazed attention, there was something almost ritualistic in the careful way Cassius closed the heavy double door.

"The screw piece was new," Cassius said deliberately, "and we found the pipe-maker who put it in. Down on Astor Place in Manhattan. He remembered the pipe. It belonged to one of his best customers, a heavy pipe-smoker. We found him."

Hyer, coursing the interminable dimensions of his new dilemma, had no comment.

"When we found the guy that owned the meer-schaum," Cassius continued, "he owned up he'd rented this room. Only he said it was two years ago. You'd expect him to say a thing like that, wouldn't you, now?"

Hyer shrugged.

"We didn't bother with it much," Cassius said carefully, "until along about noon the pipe-maker called up and said he'd found his exact record of fixing the pipe. This morning he couldn't find it. He called up and said he fixed the pipe—*two years ago last Wednesday*. It hadn't been smoked since, yet this chap that owns it, he's a heavy pipe-smoker."

The Lieutenant's voice, Hyer noticed with fresh distress, while low and unaccented, had extraordinary carrying power.

"What do you make of it?" Hyer asked.

"What do *you* make of it?" But without giving Hyer time to answer, Cassius plodded on. "This Robert How—he's a young actor, or radio announcer, or something—he says he left a trunk at Miss Doudy's two years ago. He says the clothes we found here in the room and the pipe, they were in the trunk he left here at Miss Doudy's.

"Then a little while ago we got another telephone call, Hyer. It was a tip. Most tips they come from cranks, and we don't pay much attention to them. But this didn't sound like a crank. Do you want to know what it was, Hyer?"

"What, Lieutenant?"

"Somebody said they'd looked into this room through the window about eleven o'clock last night—or maybe it was a little later; they said when the last show let out in the movie over there—and anyway— Well, they said there was a girl in the room, Hyer. It was a girl's room." Cassius paused. "We got here a quarter-past one. It was a man's room then." Pause. "I've heard of rooms changing sex," Cassius said slowly, "but only when somebody helped 'em."

Hyer shook his head. "You lost me in all that, Lieutenant."

"How did it happen you came in here last night a little while after we started working, Hyer?"

"I was visiting Molloy. He asked me to come with him when you phoned him."

(The murk of Hyer's retreat was shot with one instant gleam of satisfaction. Between this workmanlike police lieutenant and the ambitious District Attorney lay a feud whose roots struck deep into party difference, but whose fruit was that of personal malice. Cassius, Hyer could see, was quick to resent this implied slight.)

"So Molloy thought we weren't good enough to do this job?" Cassius asked, and his tone was sharp.

The double door opened. "Hyer happened to be with me," Decker Molloy said wearily. "I thought he might be interested, Lieutenant. That's all."

Cassius looked with stolid eyes at the District Attorney. "Interested enough to come back again this afternoon, wasn't he? I wonder why."

"I was curious," Hyer said. "It looked like an interesting case. It's turning out to be one."

"You wouldn't know anything about this girl, Hyer?"

"Me?"

"Great Scott, Lieutenant," Molloy burst out, "how could Hyer know anything about her? Hyer didn't hear of the case until you called me." His haggard eyes under the tufted brows shifted desperately from Cassius to Hyer and back. "If you must know, I asked Hyer to meet me here this afternoon because I wasn't satisfied with the way you're handling things."

Cassius considered this carefully. His strong seamed face was expressionless. He said, "I guess I'll be going now, Mr. Molloy."

"What did you come for?" Molloy asked. He was trembling.

"I didn't come to be insulted by a courthouse punk."

The District Attorney lunged forward.

Hyer caught his arm, struggled with him.

Cassius turned and walked deliberately out the front door.

Molloy grew quiet. His breath rasped in his throat. He stumbled and would have fallen except for Hyer's support.

Hyer, who had been on the point of a barbed comment, looked at the man's suffering face, said quietly, "You need a drink. Come back here and sit down." ·

Ten minutes later Hyer left the house.

Across the street and a little to the left, a thin man in a gray sweater was working at the engine of a black Ford sedan. He straightened up from under the hood, looked casually at Hyer. Then he bent to his work again.

Hyer walked to the avenue, turned to his right, crossed the avenue at an angle, continued two blocks, bought a newspaper and two packages of cigarettes at a stationery store, and started back to the house by a leisurely circuitous route.

His pace was that of a man out for a stroll in the quiet, leaf-scented April afternoon. The sun was hot, the air moist, rich with the promise of spring. At one corner, Hyer waited while school children trooped across the intersection under the watchful eye of a ninth-grader in a white Sam Browne belt.

Several times he stepped off the sidewalk to let small skaters clatter past. He stood for a moment eying a game of marbles, leaned on a fence and watched two men struck out in a sand-lot baseball game.

Approaching the mottled stone house along Abbey Street, he passed a coupé which bore a small plate identifying it as rented from a drive-it-yourself agency. At the wheel sat Eben Klim. Farther along, the thin man in the sweater still worked patiently at his uncovered engine.

Thirty seconds after he had passed Klim, Hyer was let into the house by Della Doudy.

He had been followed every step of the way by a man with a light gray topcoat over his arm, a gray fedora hat, and admirable talent.

13

AT four-thirty, Henry Hyer stood at the front door of the stone house, peering moodily out through the small trefoil window. A short distance up the street, Eben Klim waited in the rented coupé. In the other direction, just visible beyond the corner of the theater building, stood the black Ford, its sweatered custodian working patiently at something under the upraised hood. The man stepped back, wiped his hands on a rag, climbed in at the wheel, and ran the starter. Then he got out and went back to work.

Although he could not see it from where he stood, Hyer knew that one of the exit doors of the theater was half-open on the alley at the side of the house, and that inside the door a man in a gray fedora hat and a gray topcoat could be seen sitting.

Klim waited patiently in the rented coupé. The amateur mechanic worked patiently at his engine across the street. The watcher in the theater sat patiently in his propped-open door.

Never, Hyer thought, had the world been given such a dogged display of patience.

The late afternoon had grown dark with the approach of a storm. Under a low overcast, the air was pent-up and stifling. Passers-by went swiftly, with anxious glances at the drooping sky. Girls hurried homeward carrying open newspapers ready to be snatched above their heads when the rain broke.

A touch on his arm caused Hyer to start nervously. He said, "Oh, you."

Beside him in the murk of the hall was Della Doudy. The bracelets on her stocky forearm were silent. Today her small perfectly modeled ears, naked against a trim upswept coiffure, wore rhinestone clips in the shape of arrows.

"Hank," Della said in an anxious bass whisper, "what are we going to do?"

"I'll think of something. By the time it gets dark I can—" Hyer stopped.

The man working at the Ford's vitals had wiped his hands again. But this time, instead of getting into the car, he stood a moment staring at the rented coupé fifty yards behind. As Hyer watched, he walked to the coupé, leaned on the door and talked briefly to Eben Klim.

Hyer held his breath.

The rented coupé started, moved reluctantly along in front of the house. Hyer saw Klim look toward the veranda. Then he was gone. The mechanic went patiently back to his tinkering.

Della tugged at Hyer's shoulder, trying to lift herself to see through the trefoil window. "What's the matter?" she demanded.

"We just lost the first round to Cassius," Hyer said cheerfully. "Well, let's go back to training camp." He linked arms with his short hostess, started along the hall —and brought up like a rider who might inadvertently lasso a pillar.

"No, you don't, darling," Della whispered. One dainty hand caught his vest, turned him toward her with the gentleness of Man Mountain Dean drawing an opponent into the airplane spin. "I thought of something in there just now. I wonder if *you've* thought of it."

"Probably," Hyer said. He was straightening his vest. "If it's unpleasant."

"It's unpleasant enough."

Hyer's hands, busy at his jacket collar, were abruptly still. He looked down at the small solid woman with the rhinestone clips in her dainty ears. "What, Della?"

For an instant she seemed uncomfortable. She glanced toward the end of the hall and the closed living-room door. "We've been talking about—what happened to Deck Molloy's kid brother," she said rapidly, "as if it had to have happened *after* Madeira came in and said she'd seen a man at the window."

Again Hyer turned to walk away. Again Della spun him to face her.

"Had it occurred to you, Henry Hyer, that it might have happened *before* she came in there and told us? Had that occurred to you? That Reed was already lying there dead when you and Madeira went out? That she made it up about the window being open?"

Hyer patted her cheek. He said softly, "It took you longer than I thought it would, Della." This time he did not turn away. His fingers on her cheek slipped back to tweak the lobe of one tiny ear. "Once before," he whispered, "you made a little mistake about a client of mine. Remember, dear?"

Her eyes filled suddenly with tears. Her small mouth quivered. She stood, unmoving, and watched Hyer walk back and disappear through the living-room door. She put a trembling hand to her ear, withdrew it, stared at her reddened finger tips.

Then as blood dripped from the gash bitten deep by the rhinestone clip, Della Doudy whirled and ran upstairs.

The three in the living room were precisely as Hyer had left them five minutes earlier when inaction had sent him prowling restlessly to the front door.

Madeira knelt on a sofa against one window, her arm along its back, her chin on her arm, staring across the alley at the half-opened theater exit where the watcher sat.

Decker Molloy leaned with his elbows on the mantelpiece, his back to the shadowy room, his temples in his
hands. Pedro Cordero sat comfortably in a corner, a
cigar with a long undisturbed ash in his hand. It was
apparent that the cigar had not moved since Hyer went
out.

Cordero alone turned to look at Hyer. In the darken-
ing room his red beard was black. "Well," he asked
jovially, "is the envelopment still in progress, Colonel?"
His teeth showed.

"Progressing," Hyer said. "One of Cassius' men just
set us a brand-new problem."

Madeira turned quickly toward him.

"Splendid." Cordero laughed. "Anything but monot-
ony. What problem, amigo?"

"Logistics."

Molloy's shoulders had twitched when Cordero
laughed. He swung about to face the Venezuelan. His
hair was untidy, the heavy eyebrows splotches of black
against the pallor of his high scholarly forehead.

"Logistics?" Cordero echoed, amused. He said, "Oh.
Transportation. Then the police have already taken your
ally Klim—before we could decide how to have him—?"

"*Stop it!*" Madeira stood up, trembling. "Haven't you
done enough already? Dragging *one* innocent man into
this!"

"I told you the man had been released, Miss Thayer,"
Decker Molloy said. His voice was flat, lifeless.

"Released," Madeira said scornfully. "After every
newspaper in New York has printed his picture. 'Robert

How, an unemployed actor, alleged to have rented the
room where the murder—' "

"He's been released," Molloy broke in querulously.
"Didn't I telephone twenty minutes ago and ask? Released without bail. Don't you believe me, Miss Thayer?"

"I don't believe anyone."

Molloy shivered and turned away.

"And so," Cordero said to Hyer, "you may have been
right when you predicted we might have need to . . .
prepare another substitute for—"

"*Stop!*" Madeira walked swiftly toward the door,
brought up as Hyer caught her hand.

"Where are you going, Madeira?"

Her color was high, her eyes bright and dangerous.
"Where did Della go?"

"The front door," Hyer said softly, "is locked, Madeira."

"I'm going to find Della. I can't stay here with you
. . . ghouls." She looked hotly at Cordero, pulled her
hand from Hyer's clasp, and ran out of the room.

Hyer started to follow her, halted as the door
slammed. The sound was shocking in the silent house.
Molloy, standing now at the window, whirled and then
collapsed into a chair.

"Ghouls," Cordero said thoughtfully. "Um. Despoilers of graves." His white teeth showed. "Quite the con-
trary . . . what, Hyer?" He laughed. The cylinder of
gray ash on the cigar he held was steady and unbroken.
"Shall we run over the list again? Frankly, I must admit

that Miss Doudy becomes more and more attractive as an—"

"If you mention her name again," Molloy interrupted shrilly, "I'll—I'll . . ." He had started to rise. Now he sank back.

"Ah, that is better," Cordero said genially. "You have finally realized, have you, my friend, that you are in no position to make threats? Excellent judgment. Better judgment, I might say, than it has been my fortune to find among government officials."

Hyer lighted a cigarette. For an instant flame etched deeply the lines about his eyes and mouth. He sat down near the door, stretched his legs out, let his arms hang, relaxed.

Cordero shifted his attention from Molloy to Hyer, moving his chair slightly. The ash dropped from his cigar, leaving the coal a glowing disk.

"In fact," Cordero continued, "by far the most diverting aspect of our little affair—to me—is the extraordinary dilemma in which the District Attorney finds himself. I could not have planned it more adroitly—if I had had its planning, that is." He laughed. "You agree with me, don't you, Hyer? Surely no man in your profession can have any respect left for *políticos?*"

Cordero waited. When Hyer said nothing, he laughed again, loudly this time. "As for myself, I should have made a splendid anarchist. I could not, of course, go about waving my fists and shouting nihilist slogans. You see, I am a cautious philosopher. I have always admired the sage who said, *si philosophus tacuisses.* If you are a

philosopher, for God's sake keep your mouth shut."
Cordero laughed.

Molloy leaned forward and dropped his head in his
hands.

"Then why do I make so free with my *confiteor fidei*
now?" Cordero asked. "I'll tell you, Hyer. Every man
has an appetite for discussion—for dialectics. In me that
appetite—like the physical appetites—is abnormally
urgent.

"When I have silently observed the stupidities of our
elected officials for a time, I become fairly ravenous for
a chance to express my contempt for them. Often I have
been reduced to long and furious walks in the open
country when I would shout and argue with myself for
hours at a time where no one could overhear and be
scandalized.

"You would have thought me quite mad if you had
seen me on such a cathartic ramble. (I pay you the com-
pliment, Hyer, of assuming you do not believe me mad
here in this room.) But, to be truthful, it was a mean
and unsatisfying device. I have not the stamina of the
cynic Diogenes. In most things I find I need an audience
—or at least a partner.

"And here," Cordero said with high enthusiasm, waving his hand at the room, "I have the ideal audience—if
a somewhat passive partner in the enterprise. Here is a
bright and aspiring young District Attorney—the very
mailed fist of government—reduced by a succession of
accidents to that most inevitable and tragic product of
human society, the hunted suspect. And of all indict-

ments, the one hanging by a spider's thread above Molloy is the most completely, most perfectly, hateful—fratricide.".

Cordero paused. The room was silent. Molloy's shoulders jerked.

"I have no doubt that Attorney Molloy would make almost any sacrifice to drag me before the criminal bar as a dangerous alien." Cordero paused again and looked at Molloy's bowed head before he turned to Hyer. "*Almost* any sacrifice. But Molloy knows that to do this would be to stumble forward *with* me as surely as if manacles linked us. For to accuse me of any crime whatsoever—of any crime at all, mind you—would be to turn me into the busiest vulture that ever nagged at mortal liver. For then—bit by bit—I should tell what I know about *him*. And I know far, far too much.

"I know, for example, that Decker Molloy was in this house, hiding upstairs in a bedroom while we sat and chatted with Miss Doudy last night. Under your adroit questioning, Hyer, he has admitted that fact before all of us. Though it was perhaps a little crude of you, Hyer, to hint that I had seen him steal out while you and Madeira were outside investigating—"

"You've nothing but a match to prove I was here," Molloy broke in. "I can deny—"

"And can you deny that you arranged for Madeira to leave her position in the bank, arranged for her to come here, to lodge in the room where your brother—"

"I was desperate," Molloy said brokenly. "After you and she came to see me Friday night, Reed showed me the picture in the watch—boasted he was going to find and kill that girl. . . . I knew he was hiding from something. . . . I was—"

"And can you deny," Cordero asked sternly, "that you refused to own him as your brother when you saw him lying dead on the floor with his—"

"Don't—*don't!*" Molloy gasped. He stood up unsteadily. His shoulders were shaking. He put his hands to his face, lurched toward the door, upsetting one table and knocking an alabaster vase from another.

Hyer was on his feet. He caught Molloy at the door, led him into the hall. "Where are you going?" Hyer asked quietly.

"Where can I go?" Molloy's hands dropped from his face. Another soundless sob convulsed him. "Reed . . ." he whispered. "Reed."

"You'd better lie down," Hyer said. He took Molloy's arm, led him to the stairs, and motioned for Molloy to precede him.

The second-floor hall was in almost complete darkness. Hyer took Molloy's arm again, listened. There was a murmur from behind a closed door to his left. Hyer turned to the right, opened another door at random. He drew Molloy into a twilit bedroom. It was the room where Molloy had waited the night before.

The District Attorney sat on the bed like a docile child. "I keep seeing him, Hyer," he whispered. "Seeing him—seeing his face. . . . He was a handsome boy, Hyer. . . . He carried the censer at Mass. . . . Once at Christmas he had pneumonia and we thought he was going to—" He dropped face down on the pillow. "Reed," he sobbed, "Reed . . . Reed."

Hyer waited a minute until the other man was quiet.

He went out of the room and across the hall to the door where there was the murmur of voices. He rapped lightly and went in.

Madeira was sitting in a window seat, silhouetted against the rapidly failing light. Della Doudy lay in a chaise longue. She wore a white dressing gown.

Neither Della nor Madeira spoke.

Hyer walked to the chaise longue. He said, "I've a job for you, Della."

No reply.

Lightning flashed, bringing the room into sharp detail. In the instant brilliance, Della Doudy's greenish eyes glowed like a cheetah's.

Thunder exploded.

Hyer bent over the chaise longue. "I want you to stay with Molloy."

Della sat up. "Stay with Deck? What has he—?"

"Nothing yet," Hyer said. "That's why I want you to stay with him."

She walked rapidly before him to the door. Hyer turned, said, "Madeira."

She was on her feet. She came swiftly toward him, was on the point of passing him when Hyer caught her. "Where are you going, Madeira?"

"To clear this whole thing up." She tried to release her arm. "Let me go," she commanded.

"Not unless you promise to stay here in the house."

"Let me go!"

"Not if you—"

"*Let—me—go!*"

Hyer caught her other arm. They faced each other in the lightning's pulses.

Below there was a shout, "Hyer! Oh, Hyer!"

Madeira kicked at his kneecap, jerked her arms, tried to free herself.

Hyer said softly, "When you can be a good girl, I'll let you out." He picked her up, carried her, struggling, to the chaise longue, dropped her, sprinted to the door before she could leap to her feet, slipped the key from its hole, went out, and locked the door quickly behind him.

As the bolt went home, Hyer could feel the knob rattling. He put his lips to the edge of the panel. "Will you take orders?"

A pause.

"Will you, Madeira?"

"No."

Hyer said, "I'll come back after while."

There was another shout from Cordero. "I say, Hyer!"

Hyer went swiftly to the room where he had left Molloy. He could see Della Doudy, a white ministrant, leaning over the bed.

As he ran downstairs, the rain came with the rush of primeval flood, and with the rain the wind howling.

14

CORDERO was waiting for Hyer in the hall. "Didn't you hear me call you? Where's Madeira, Hyer?"

"I heard you."

"This is our chance to get Madeira away from here," Cordero said excitedly. "The police will never see us in this storm. Where is she?"

"They'll see us. She's upstairs. Standing in a corner."

"I'll talk to her." Cordero vaulted up the stairs.

Thunder crashed incessantly now. Rain broke in solid sheets against the door. In the lightning, Hyer could see small trickles of water squirming across the threshold and along the floor. He waited at the foot of the stairs.

Presently Cordero returned. "The door's locked, Hyer!" he shouted above the din of the storm.

Hyer said, "I know. I locked it."

"Why, for God's sake?" Cordero seized Hyer's shoulder, his grip not gentle. "Why did you lock her in?"

Hyer shook off the big man's hand, and walked back to the living room.

Cordero followed him.

"Cassius," Hyer said hoarsely, "put his men out there to wait for whoever comes out of this house. He's doing it the long way because he hates Molloy. He wants to ruin Molloy. He's waiting to see if a girl comes out of this house—along with Molloy."

"But what—?"

"Wait till dark." Hyer drew the heavy drapes over the rain-slashed windows. "There's no hurry." He lighted a floor lamp, turned to face Cordero, who was standing in the middle of the room. "Cassius isn't hurrying—yet."

Cordero was grave. "Then you think the police suspect . . . Madeira?"

"They're waiting," Hyer said grimly. "They know the room was changed."

"That was your responsibility."

Hyer, about to retort, caught Cordero's eyes and shrugged. He said. "The damage is done," and sat down.

Cordero also sat, facing Hyer. He drew out a cigar. "Then it must be repaired," he said softly.

Hyer studied his cigarette case.

"In brief," Cordero continued, "we must find a new

. . . candidate for the attention of the police. Before their own enthusiasm leads them into dangerous ground. Right?"

Hyer grunted. He looked toward the hallway. The immediate fury of the storm was already spent, the rain slackening to a steady downpour. Hyer got up and walked lightly to the door. Decker Molloy was coming downstairs. Molloy halted on the bottom step, supported himself on the newel post, and stared at Hyer. Then, without speaking, he started to the door.

"Molloy!" Hyer called.

The District Attorney hesitated.

Della Doudy leaned over the banister. She was hooking the gray frock she had worn the day before. Where the rhinestone clip had been there was now a white patch. "Hank," she called, seeing Hyer come into the hall, "Deck doesn't know what he's doing." Her fingers flew at the hooks over one sheathed hip.

Hyer went to Molloy. "Go back upstairs," he said in the persuasive voice one would use with a child. "I'll have Cordero take you home after while."

Molloy shivered. He turned and went obediently up toward Della.

Hyer waited until the two had disappeared. Then he returned to Cordero. He said, "Molloy's breaking up."

Cordero fingered his thick red beard. The diamond glinted. "Perhaps I was a little too drastic in my act. By the way," he added quickly, "I hope you weren't taken in by it, Hyer."

"I knew you were acting." Hyer sat down where he could look through the open hall door.

"My harangue was intended merely to—"

"I know. You wanted to soften him up."

"Yes. By showing him how helpless he is to make things unpleasant for any of us."

"He's impressed," Hyer said shortly.

"Good. Now for our problem." Cordero leaned back and blew a series of rapid smoke rings. "I suppose we may as well discard Miss Doudy, considering the attitude you and the District Attorney take toward her . . . candidacy."

"And considering the fact she could hang us all."

"Um." Cordero stared at the ceiling. "We come back to Klim, don't we?"

"Do we?"

"Consider, amigo. Klim was aboard the raft with Reed and John Thayer. Klim knew of the existence of the watch, felt he had an interest in it. When Reed deserted him in the hospital in Charleston, Klim was resentful."

"Was he?" Hyer asked. "I guess I didn't know about that."

Cordero frowned. "But didn't you tell me yourself? Or," quickly, "did I imagine it? *Qué importa?* . . . At any rate, we can establish the fact that Klim made contact with Reed in New York, that Klim was in Highbridge—"

"Can we?"

Cordero waved his hand. "You *did* tell me that. We

can establish the fact that Klim discovered the watch
this morning in Reed's hotel room—" He sat up, his
black eyes suddenly bright. "Klim could have put the
watch there himself, Hyer."

Hyer said, "Go on. You can make an airtight case
for Klim—except for one unimportant detail."

"And there is the fact that Klim does not know Reed's
real identity," Cordero continued. "That will recommend Klim highly to the District Attorney, who must
prosecute the case. In prosecuting Klim, Molloy runs a
minimum risk of incriminating himself."

"Or . . . Madeira?" Hyer asked.

Cordero drew deeply on his cigar. "Um. You say that
Klim knows the picture in the watch to be that of Madeira—and knows that Reed threatened Madeira's life?"
He was silent a moment. "But that alone would scarcely
be crucial evidence. The essential thing is not that Madeira be kept clear of the case as a whole, but merely
that she have no connection with this—this house of am-
bush. Right?"

"So far." Hyer was watching Cordero intently now.

"And Molloy will do everything he can to keep Madeira from being associated with the house, right? Since
his own safety depends on that." He waited for an answer, glanced at Hyer. "What do you say, amigo?"

"Go on."

"Very well. We place in the hands of the District
Attorney all details involving Klim. He has Klim arrested. Klim tells a confused story, calls on you for con-
firmation. You admit that you arranged for Klim to

come up here and watch the house this afternoon. You explain that you were already suspicious of Klim and wished to see how he would react in the neighborhood of the crime."

Cordero, excited now, leaned forward gesturing with his cigar. "Here is what we shall say happened. Listen." His black eyes glittered. "Last night, Klim followed Reed to this house. He followed Reed to the window. Reed stepped back when he saw Madeira looking at him —stepped back and collided with Klim. There was a struggle. Klim killed Reed. But just then the patrons of the theater began passing on the sidewalk, and in terror Klim tumbled Reed's body into the room through the open window." Cordero tapped the ash from his cigar. "Do you follow me, amigo?"

Hyer nodded slowly. "I . . . follow you."

"Klim took the watch from Reed's pocket—after climbing into the room himself and closing and locking the window." Cordero stopped. "By Jove, that *could* have happened, Hyer. There was time enough when none of us was near the room." At the expression on Hyer's face, he shrugged. "*Pues bien.* We shall say that Klim found the trunk in the closet. He scattered the unfortunate actor's effects about as a blind, crept out of the house, and escaped—*with the watch.*

"Perfect, eh, amigo? With the watch, which he had taken from Reed's pocket. This morning he put the watch in Reed's hotel room, came for you, and then pretended to discover it there." Cordero leaned back. "Well?"

"Except for the fact that Klim spent the night dead-drunk in his own hotel room."

Cordero rumpled his beard impatiently. He frowned. "Can Klim prove that?"

Hyer nodded. "By a room clerk."

"Um. But if something were to happen to the room clerk—"

"That kind are indestructible. They have to be."

Cordero sighed. "Then you do not favor Klim in the rôle of . . . understudy?" He sighed again. "It would simplify much."

For a quarter of an hour the room was silent. Hyer rose once and went to the window. He turned off the lamp and parted the heavy drapes. It was quite dark now. Rain still fell, a steady drumming downpour, but the wind had died. Hyer let the curtains fall into place and relighted the lamp. He went to the hall door, listened, and returned to his chair.

"If there were only ourselves to consider," Cordero began at last, "I would say to chance it with Klim and damn the risk. But for Madeira's sake—" He turned his cigar carefully, then with a ruthless flick sent the long ash flying.

"As for myself, Hyer, I prefer bold risks. It is in my line. No true Venezuelan ever forgets that somewhere in his ancestry there is the high blood of the Carib. Through my own mother I like to think that I can trace my family back to genuine Carib stock.

"Let me tell you something about my Carib ancestors, Hyer. You may listen if you like, or you can let me be merely a sounding surf to help you concentrate. They were invincible warriors—my Carib sires. And their women, too. For the Carib women were the true Amazons. They fought with even greater dash and ferocity than their sons. It is told that they sliced off—each for herself—the right breast to have greater freedom for the sword arm.

"They ranged the hemisphere from Florida to the deep jungles, these Caribs, and everywhere they were unchallenged masters—until the Spaniards came. No, even *after* the Spaniards came. For in them the bloody conquistadors at first found their match. Do I bore you, Hyer?"

Hyer, staring intently at the other, shook his head.

"They were the world's finest horsemen—yes, horsemen, believe me, *caballeros*. For the Caribs alone in this new world were not frightened of the Spaniard's horses. They were frightened of nothing above hell. They found the sturdy Spanish Arab perfectly suited to the vast Orinoco campaña and so expert were they as trainers, that horse, rider, and weapon became one deadly lightning-swift machine.

"They were the inventors of camouflage. A painted Carib was as invisible as a wraith. They conceived poison gas, sealing toxic fumes in clay balls and then hurling these with disastrous results, believe me, among squads of the cuirassed despoilers.

"Their arrows, tipped with deadly strychnine—curare is a novelist's plaything—they shot from bows as long as a man. With one arrow a Carib man could shatter the

bole of a ten-year oak, and they could aim with hair-
fine accuracy from any position."

Cordero laughed. "It was no accident that the Spanish invaders scurried to claim Sebastian for their patron
saint—as one perhaps more familiar with the effects of
archery than his colleagues. And they were no less invincible on the water, these Carib legions.

"Across the sea they named, the Caribs would dart in
their *flecheras*—war canoes with the speed of torpedos
and each manned by as many as a hundred warriors. In
fleets of two hundred, they would attack the sluggish
galleons and sting whole flotillas to death before the
clumsy cannon could be laid."

Hyer was leaning back, hands clasped behind his
head. But his eyes were alert, intent on the man before
him. He made no move as Cordero paused and relighted
his cigar.

"In fact," Cordero continued, "so bold were they that
on one occasion two Carib fighters allowed themselves
to be captured by a slaver and battened below decks
with a herd of spiritless Indians. When they put in at a
Cuban port, the ship's officers went ashore and eight
men were left in charge of the caravel.

"The captives were chained below the main deck in
a space only high enough for a man to sit. When the
two Caribs were sure that most of the guards were gone,
they assumed command over the other Indians—who
rightly regarded them as masters—ordered every man to
lie on his back, brace his feet against the timbers overhead, and thrust in concert at a signal.

"The dry-rotted planking buckled upward and burst, the slaves surged out, killed the eight guards, and then under command of the two Caribs sailed the Spanish ship back to the Orinoco. On another occasion– But I must be boring you, Hyer."

"Not at all," Hyer said quickly–so quickly that Cordero glanced at him. "Boring me? No, indeed."

Cordero waved his hand. "Enough of anecdotes. But you see, Hyer, why I am proud of my stock."

Hyer nodded. "I see."

"Now to get back to our problem–"

"I've thought of something," Hyer said.

"Ah, then I did help you concentrate."

"You did." Hyer sat up. He said, speaking slowly and distinctly, "You may be right. I mean about trying the experiment–with Klim."

"Yes?" Cordero lifted his eyebrows. "From something I said–"

"An idea came to me. Something I'd missed before."

The two men looked at each other intently. Cordero's black eyes were brilliant.

"If you would tell me, amigo," he began, "what it was I said which–"

"That might spoil the whole thing," Hyer said easily.

"By keeping your own council last night," Cordero reminded him, "we are now *in* this dilemma."

"And by keeping my own council, I may be able to get at least Madeira out of it. That was the bargain, wasn't it?"

Cordero touched his beard. "For–"

"Twenty thousand dollars." Hyer stood up. "I want you to take Molloy home. If the police follow you, it doesn't make any difference. Deliver him at home and then go on to New York if you—"

"Madeira will—?"

"Madeira will stay here."

Cordero smiled. "I shall come back here . . . Hen-ry."

"All right. But I want to get Molloy home right away. Come."

"Madeira will go with me," Cordero said.

"And walk into Cassius' trap?" Hyer demanded angrily.

"Um. But— Wait, why cannot you take Molloy? In my car?"

"I can't drive a car. Della can chaperon us. Come on."

As they started upstairs, Cordero laid his hand on Hyer's arm. "You know what you are doing—this time?"

"I knew what I was doing last night. I didn't put that meerschaum pipe in the drawer."

Cordero sighed. "Unhappy error. And my error, of course. Yes. *Pues bien.*" . . . He followed Hyer up the staircase.

15

DECKER MOLLOY had recovered but little when he left the house with Cordero. In his eyes there was still a vacant, helpless look, and his step as Cordero guided him to the door was that of a man sleepwalking.

Della Doudy walked at the other side of Molloy, speaking to him quietly, reassuringly. "You'll be all right, Deck. Nice hot bath . . . drink . . . long sleep. . . ." She wore a gray cape and a small uptilted black hat. At the door she stepped aside as Molloy went out with Cordero. Then while the two men moved across the veranda she ran lightly back to Hyer, who stood at the foot of the stairs.

"See what you've done to Deck," she said fiercely. "You'd no right to do that to him. He went through hell last night, didn't he? He's only human. You've got to let him alone now—hear!" She clenched one dainty fist and beat Hyer's arm. *"Let—Deck—alone."* There was a desperate urgency in her greenish eyes, a light that was at once imperative and pleading.

Hyer said, "They're waiting for you, Della."

She caught his sleeve. "Hank," she whispered, "please leave Deck alone—for a little while. His own kid brother, Hank." . . . Her grip on his sleeve relaxed. She touched Hyer's hand humbly. "Hank—" She waited. "Deck's a good guy, Hank. He's weak, that's all. His own worst enemy. He's been through hell ever since Reed came back—keeping his mother from knowing Reed *was* back. Hank," softly, "it would kill his mother to know . . . all this. Can't we give her a break? She's a sweet thing. You've got a mother, Hank," she pleaded.

Hyer was silent.

"Damn you!" she cried. "I hate you. I hate all of you. I hate this house. I'm not coming back. I'll rot before I'll ever set foot in this damned house again."

She struck Hyer in the face with her open hand, turned, and ran out across the veranda.

Hyer watched her overtake Cordero and Molloy at the curb, saw her help Molloy into Cordero's car. The car moved away. A moment later the Ford, whose patient guardian had worked so long at his engine, followed.

Hyer murmured, "One," absently. He closed and

locked the front door, went upstairs, listened for a moment outside the door which he had bolted on Madeira. "It won't be long now," he said, his lips at the crack. "Will you behave if I let you out?"

He waited, drew a long breath, straightened his shoulders, and went quickly downstairs like a man who, after a yawing indecisive period, is ready at last to assert himself.

After a search, he found the telephone concealed in a lacquered cabinet beside the chair where he had sat listening to Cordero. He perched on the arm of the chair, squinted thoughtfully at the alabaster angels below the mantelpiece, lifted the telephone, and dialed Operator.

"I want Highbridge police headquarters," he said.

When the phone at the other end began to ring, Hyer added in a low confidential tone, "And you busybodies listening in might as well get your sharp little pencils out. . . . Hello, this is Henry Hyer. I want Lieutenant Cassius." . . . He fumbled for a cigarette, snapped his case shut, and put it away again. The light picked out tiny bright drops of perspiration at his temple.

"Hello, Cassius. Hyer. . . . Still where you left me. I've a proposition for you. . . . Yes, it's a simple one. You take Bright Eyes away from the kitchen door of that movie palace across the alley, let me walk out of here without a kite string on me, and I'll guarantee to tie up your case and hand it to you. . . . Because I want to do it *my* way. . . . Even as a kid I was selfish, Lieutenant. . . . Well, I'll tell you this much, and you can go to work on it.

"Somewhere in New York City or New York harbor," Hyer said, speaking slowly and carefully, "you'll find a seafaring man six feet six inches or so tall and left-handed. He's probably off a merchantman, and he's probably a deck or engine officer. . . . All right, all right, so it's vague. So was the description of Hauptmann vague. But I'll tell you this: Locate all the six-foot-plus maritime southpaws who've been in New York in the last twenty-four hours, and you'll have a confession in this Abbey Street case within—"

He listened. "What *I'm* going to do is my own business. Will you pull off your bird dog and let me do it? . . . Why *should* you?" angrily. "Because I'm offering you the best bargain you ever got. Do me one small favor—and I hand you a case that'll give you two strikes on an inspectorship. . . . What if you *don't?*" Hyer's mouth contracted. "In that case, I'll have to do the whole thing myself—take credit for it myself—and leave you the laughing stock of every precinct house from Boston to—"

Again he listened. "Be reasonable, Lieutenant. What good will it do you to keep me chained up here? Everybody else has cleared out. Molloy's gone. Miss Doudy isn't coming back here—swears she'll never step inside the door again. If you want to tie up taxpayers' money keeping a point on *me*, that's your— . . . Because," Hyer said testily, "I've got my pride. I never walked out of a house in my life with an official tin can tied to my— . . . That's right, and I don't intend to now. How about it? Take your beagle off me, round up those left-handed merchant marines, give me until tomorrow night, and you'll have your confession." . . . He drew a long breath. . . . "All right, the sooner you— . . . Am I working for *Molloy?*" in amazement. "My God, no!"

He put the telephone away, muttered, "Working for —Molloy!" disgustedly, and stood up. There was a nervous eagerness in his manner now. He looked toward the hall, and the preoccupied expression in his eyes relaxed. He took a step toward the door, stopped.

For a moment he stood, listening intently. About him the house was silent. Even the rain had stopped. Then he heard it again, the ghost of a sound, as if something were happening in the wall behind the chair he had just quitted.

Hyer tiptoed back and knelt beside the chair. In the wall at its back was a grilled space, apparently part of the heating system. Making no sound, he wedged himself in and put his ear to the grille. For a moment the stillness was unbroken. Then there was a faint tinkle as of loose glass disturbed by a stealthy foot. A moment later a board scraped.

Someone was moving in the basement below.

Hyer stood up. He looked from the grille to the chair and back to the grille, while his lips tightened and anticipation lighted in his eyes. Then, walking lightly across the deep Oriental rug, he went to the dining-room door, felt his way without making a sound past the table on which he had sat the night before clasping his stocky reluctant hostess, entered the dark kitchen, and began exploring cautiously for the cellar door.

He did not dare light a match. The first door he opened brought spices eddying out, the second the smell of sweeping compound. Patiently he went on, charting the wall with his finger tips, skirting the stove, colliding with a refrigerator, until he came to a third door. This was locked, but the key was in place.

Gently he turned the key, muffled the latch mechanism under pressure on the knob, and drew the door open. The odors which met him this time were cellar odors, coming on a light draft of moist night air. He could hear a faint drip.

An agony of apprehension seized him as he thought of Madeira behind another locked door on the floor above. He was on the point of abandoning this lead and returning at once to release Madeira when he heard, unmistakably now, someone moving in the cellar.

For a moment he was torn between two imperatives: one a burning urgency that drew him to a girl who was all at once as impellingly real in the silent darkness as if she stood beside him, the other an infallible certainty that the answer to Madeira's problem was but a dozen steps from him in the damp cellar.

It was not intuition but a cold and rigid logic which told Hyer that at the foot of the invisible cellar steps was a quarry that must be taken. For from the same logic came a grim conviction that if he failed now, he himself would become quarry to the other's relentless stalking. He had spoken too freely to Lieutenant Cassius within range of the grilled opening which, if it carried rustling upward, must surely have carried his words to the listener below.

From the updraft, he judged a cellar window to be open. The quarry would be making for that open window.

Hyer let himself down to the first step, the second, the third. There was the faintest lessening of the darkness, like a false dawn. On he went, stepping carefully at the supported edges of the treads to reduce the hazard of creaking.

There was no sound now. Hyer felt the smooth handrail grow slick under his palm. His groping foot struck a box lurking on one step, faltered, felt gingerly for the step below, and came to rest on concrete. He was down.

Now he could see the faint square of the open window—on the side of the house away from the theater where Cassius' watcher sat. He held his breath, strained his ears, tried by some ancient and unused sense to perceive the presence of the other. He himself, he knew, must have been invisible against the blackness of the stairs—unless he had already passed in profile before the lighter screen of the open window.

Directly behind him was the scrape of a shoe sole on wood.

But even as he tried to whirl, Hyer found himself too slow. He knew only that the arm which crashed up under his chin was wet-sleeved and guided by a ruthless skill—had only time to remember the broken neck of the man the night before.

Some buried reflex brought a choking cry to his lips
—"Madeira!"—then his breath was bursting in his throat,
a deeper darkness was engulfing him, his knees were
sagging. . . .

But in the twilight of consciousness, Hyer was aware
of a strange, incredible thing. For he found himself falling—falling through a vast illimitable nothingness—*forward*. This circumstance was so odd that for a long
time he seemed to be withdrawn at some distance,
watching himself fall, puzzled, curious, and a little
amused, for this thing was impossible.

The technique of the skilled mugger has as nice and
inevitable a protocol as that of a proper swordsman: for
a victim to pitch forward midway of the ceremony is
as gauche as for a fencer to kneel on the strip and tie
his shoelace.

Hyer's drowsy trajectory through semiconsciousness
exploded in a shattering impact. The shock of this reawakened his bruised throat to a new convulsive struggle
for breath, knocked wakefulness into his muddled mind,
snapped his paralysis.

He heard his name called, felt a shoe strike his hand—
and then Madeira was on her knees beside him, lifting
him in her arms, pressing his head to her shoulder. There
was the sound of feet running up the stairs.

"Henry!" . . . Madeira cried. "Henry!"

Gasping, Hyer drew himself up, touched her hair.
"You're—" He choked. "You're—all right, Madeira?"

"Your face is bleeding."

"Funny," Hyer gasped. "Does that—every time I—fall on it. Hurry!"

He lurched to his feet, drew Madeira up, said, "Thanks," his lips at her ear, and stumbled up the steps toward the kitchen.

They had not yet reached the head of the stairs when the sound of the front door slamming came to them.

Hyer, Madeira at his heels, raced through the dining room, across the richly cluttered living room, and along the dark hall. But at the front door he stopped, peering out through the trefoil window.

Madeira, pressing against his shoulder, asked, "What? What, Henry?"

Hyer was watching a man in a gray fedora and flying gray topcoat sprint under the dim light at the alley entrance and run diagonally back across the lawn. He passed within two feet of the veranda and disappeared.

"Hat and coat," Hyer rasped, clutching his throat.

Madeira sped away. Hyer, mopping at his bleeding face with a handkerchief, stumbled after her. But before he reached the end of the hall, the living-room light went out, and an instant later Madeira collided with him.

"I've yours, too," she said rapidly. "Here."

Hyer felt his hat dropped on his head, felt her finger tips for an instant at one bruised temple, and then they were hurrying to the front door, out of the house, across the dark veranda, down the walk together.

At the street, Hyer piloted Madeira straight across to the far sidewalk, turned to the right, and ran with her

fifty yards. They were in deep shadow here. At a clump
of shrubbery before a darkened house, Hyer stopped,
found a gate ajar in a picket fence, pushed the gate open,
and stepped through. Leaning against the fence, he drew
Madeira into the crook of one arm.

She took the handkerchief from him, touched his face
with it. Her hand was trembling.

The shrubbery dripped. Cars sped wetly past on the
avenue a half-block away.

Hyer's arm tightened about Madeira. "How did you
get there?" he whispered.

"I climbed out a window. I was furious with you."

Hyer chuckled. "Climbed out a window?"

"There was a drainpipe. But those stones, set the way
they are, make you a regular ladder. I found the cellar
window open when I got to the ground. I thought I
heard something, and waited. After while I *did* hear
something. It was you."

"Sh."

She twisted in his arm, looked back toward the house,
stiffened.

A white-topped police car had turned out of the avenue and come to a stop at the entrance to the alley. A
policeman jumped out and walked briskly to one of the
dimly lighted theater exits. He tried this, found it locked.
Just then the car's spotlight flashed on, showed the man
in the gray fedora running back the way he had come
two minutes before.

"Nice timing," Madeira murmured.

Hyer felt her shiver.

The one in the gray hat came up to the police car. There was a brief conference. All three got in. The car turned around and went back to the avenue.

"Cassius keeps his word," Hyer murmured.

"What, Henry?"

"We can start now. Ready for a walk, Madeira?"

"Are you?" quickly.

"No. But I'll feel better if we take a train from Bronxville or Albany." He turned her to face him. "The next time you save my life—"

"The next time *you* lock me in a room, Henry Hyer—"

Hyer grinned. "Entertaining future, isn't it?" He linked arms with her, marched out through the picket gate, and turned westward away from the avenue. "Once upon a time there were three bears and a little girl named Goldilocks—"

"I've heard that one. Blondes bore me."

"Cinderella?"

"Opiate for the working girl."

"As an audience," Hyer said caustically, "you can't hold a candle to Angelica."

"My literary taste was debauched at the age of seven by an Igorot witch doctor." She looked down, suited her pace to Hyer's longer stride. "But I always had a secret longing to hear the one that begins 'Once upon a time a poor but honest maiden was imprisoned by an ogre—'"

"That isn't the way I heard it," Hyer interrupted brusquely. "And anyway it doesn't have an end."

Presently she said, "But it will have an end, Henry."

"If the poor but honest maiden is a good girl and—"

"Keeps out of fights?"

Hyer said, "We—ll—you can carry a good thing too far."

Madeira laughed. "Now I know why Angelica adores you."

"The Spanish," Hyer observed, "have odd tastes." But his step grew lighter as they went on under the dripping branches.

16

IT was twenty-five minutes past seven when Madeira and Hyer got out of a cab in Bank Street.

While Hyer paid the driver, Madeira stood looking up at the lighted windows. On the third floor curtains parted and a small figure showed briefly, forehead pressed to the pane. Madeira laughed and waved.

The small figure catapulted back from the window. Faintly from within they could hear descending shouts: "Jonah—Jo—nah—Jo-o-o-o-nah!" A pan clattered below-stairs, and Jonah Hastie's white-aproned bulk surged past a window of the basement kitchen like the Genoa jib of a hurried sloop.

"Do you know," Madeira murmured as she ran up the steps at Hyer's side, "I'm becoming fond of this house."

There was a pounding down the stairs, a thump, the door flew open, and Angelica leaped into Hyer's arms.

Hyer winced as she clasped her small wiry arms about his bruised neck and buried her face in his shoulder. He patted her, said, "Well, well, what's all this?"

Angelica clutched him tighter. She whispered, "I been so afraid for you, Tío Hank. Don't scold. I try hard not to be afraid, but—*cómo se dice*—no soap."

Hyer chuckled and set her down in the hall. Madeira knelt and put her arm around Angelica, now gone suddenly shy.

Jonah appeared at the head of the basement stairs, grinning. Absently he lifted a fold of the white apron and mopped his round perspiring face. "Couldn't lemme know in time to put potatoes up to bake," he grumbled. "Oh, no. Couldn't stop in a phone booth an' gimme a—"

"I tell you they be here," Angelica cried, whirling on him. "I say seven-thirty—"

"An' you said *foh*-thirty an' *five* an' *five*-thirty an' *six* an' *six*-thirty an' *seb'm*," Jonah reminded her. "You th' mos' flexible talent for pre-diction, young lady."

"You've been expecting us since four-thirty, dear?" Madeira asked gently.

Angelica tilted her nose at Jonah. "Those firs' times I merely practice. Seven-thirty was right, no?" But as the little girl looked swiftly at Hyer again, there was the echo of a long and despairing vigil in her bright black eyes.

After Angelica and Madeira had gone up to the third floor, Jonah followed Hyer to his bedroom and helped him off with his coat. As Hyer raised his chin to loosen his tie, Jonah said, "Oh, oh," quickly. "Somebody take you, boss?" he asked, and there was deep concern in the question.

Hyer, tenderly touching his bruised jowls, grunted. He lowered his hands as Jonah examined the soiled V left by the attacker's elbow-vise.

"Mmmmmmmmmm-*hm*," Jonah murmured. "Somebody with know-how, yes, sir." He shook his head. "Pretty a muggin' as I ever—"

"You're not painting it," Hyer said testily. "You're fixing it." He moved his head, winced. "I think I've got a broken neck."

He sat on a stool in the bathroom while Jonah gently massaged salve into the twin bruises. "What happened at home?" Hyer asked.

"Phone calls all afternoon. Schultz—one at headquarters—called right after you went out. Said you gib'm a number an' wanted a name for it."

"And the name was Molloy?" Hyer asked wearily.

"Molloy? Why, no, boss. Name was Braun."

"Braun?" Hyer twisted his head and regarded Jonah sharply.

"Albert Braun. How I remember, he called up himself about twenty minutes later. Braun. That's the name."

That's what Schultz said. Then Sergeant Tooley over't
the Sixt' Precinct, he called in an'—"

"Wait a minute. What did Braun want?"

"I'm trying to tell you."

"You said Tooley from the Sixth Precinct—"

"In the interest of economy, I was exterminatin' two
birds with one projectile. Braun an' Tooley bofe had
th' same message to give you, boss."

"Oh."

"That's right. Say nex' time you fix up a practical
joke for somebody—"

"So Braun took me seriously, did he?" Hyer grinned.
"He stopped over at the Sixth Precinct this noon and
asked why the police were looking for his car, did he?
Well, well." He frowned. "But are you sure Schultz
said the gun belonged to Braun?"

"Gun? What gun, boss?"

Hyer said, "Skip it. Other calls?"

"Klim. 'Bout a quarter to five. Say if you call I'm to
tell you he had to take back the car he rented. Say he
was going to hire a taxicab and try that way."

Hyer nodded. "I saw him take the car back. What
else?"

"Al Jocelyn wants to know you comin' up to dinner
Friday night. Kennel people call up an' say they got
that Doberman puppy you ordered f'Angelica."

"Female?"

"Boss," Jonah said earnestly, "I been meanin' to speak
to you about that. You sure you want to clutter this
place up with any more of th' opposite persuasion?"

When Hyer did not reply at once, Jonah said, "Oh, oh," softly.

"What's that?"

"Angelica's sure took to her, yes, sir. Way little Angelica carried on this evenin'—"

"Did you tell her about the Doberman?" Hyer demanded.

"Doberman? What Doberman, boss?" Jonah's eyes in his round black face were wide and innocent.

Master and man stared at each other. Slowly both grinned. "My, my," Jonah murmured, "think of you gettin'—"

"All right," Hyer said brusquely, "you've done enough thinking." He stood up. "Did you press my—? Hello, look who's here!"

Angelica ran into the room and hugged him about the middle, hiding her face in his shirt, her small shoulders quivering. Hyer smoothed her straight black hair and grinned at Jonah.

He said, "That's the trouble with these Basques. No emotion in 'em. For instance, even if we were talking about a Doberman puppy with big floppy paws and a wet nose—"

Angelica lifted her face. Her black eyes were round and reverent. Her lips trembled. There were still tears on her lashes. "Tío . . . Hank . . ." she whispered. She caught her breath, said in a rush, "*Entonces es verdad lo de el* puppy *que yo puedo tener, el* puppy *que pedía a Dios todas las noches* . . ."

"See?" Hyer said to Jonah. "You can't get any closer

to 'em than a dictionary." He sat on the bed, lifted a corner of Jonah's white apron, and wiped Angelica's eyes. The little girl caught his hand and pressed her forehead against it.

When Hyer came out of the small dressing room after a time, Angelica was sitting tailor-wise on his bed. She said, "See what I find today, Tío Hank."

Jonah, who was going through the door, looked over his shoulder. He said hastily, "Well, I better be getting dinner on," and quickened his pace.

"Jonah!"

Angelica, her small mouth prim, her black eyes impish, dropped into Hyer's palm the dice she held. "In the kitchen I find them—hiding in a little drawer with the foot of a hare." She looked innocently from Hyer to Jonah. "It is—*cómo se dice*—it is a game?"

"In a little drawer in the kitchen," Hyer murmured. "Why, yes, honey, a kind of a game. Like bank robbery."

Angelica frowned. "But—robbery—that is where you lose your money, no?"

"Jonah," Hyer said brightly, "shall we show Angelica?"

Jonah, gazing at the white cubes fixedly, gave a start. He turned to go again. "Gotta get dinner on now, if—"

"Jonah." Hyer beckoned with a grim finger. "All right, honey, you and I'll play and let Jonah be audience."

"But I have no money, Tío Hank."

"Jonah has. I paid him this morning. He'll let you have some."

Jonah swallowed. His unhappy glance dropped from Hyer's bland unrelenting face to the dice. Slowly he worked his hand under the apron and into his pocket.

"My, my," Hyer said as he took the folded bills and smoothed them out on the bed before Angelica. "How much have you now, baby?"

She counted. "Thirty-two dollars." She looked up eagerly. "Now what I do?"

"You lay one dollar out—like this, honey, and I lay a dollar out—like this. And then," briskly, "I take the little white things you found—like this."

Jonah sank slowly to a chair by the door, a global figure of gloom.

Presently Madeira called, "Hello, what are you people doing in there?"

"Homework," Hyer answered. "Come in."

Madeira stood in the doorway. "What in the—?"

"And now, honey," Hyer said, "I do it again and— What do you know, seven again! So I pick up your *last* dollar and—well, that's the game."

"But I have no money left," Angelica complained.

Hyer nodded. "That's the game."

"It is *not* no game. It is a thieving. I do not like it," Angelica said stoutly.

Hyer winked at Madeira. "But there's one funny thing, baby. Run get me a glass of water and I'll show you."

Jonah sighed.

Angelica scrambled off the bed and returned in a moment from the bathroom with the glass. Madeira came to sit on the bed beside Hyer. She said, "This is a new one on me."

"Watch," Hyer said. He dropped one of the dice gently into the water. It spun over and sank. He dropped the other. It turned lazily through a half-gainer.

Angelica clapped her hands.

Jonah stood up dismally. "Couldn't spare a dime for a professional man jus' lost his sole means of support, could you, boss?"

When Angelica had run out of the room after Jonah, Hyer and Madeira sat for a moment without speaking. She leaned back, swept the curtain aside, and gazed across the dark rain-freshened gardens. The windows in the house opposite were lighted. In one kitchen a man was bending over a table cranking an egg-beater. On the floor above, a man and a woman were washing dishes. The tall girl of the cerise pyjama bottoms, now quite formally gowned in black, leaned toward a mirror, fixing a flower above her ear. Through the silence came a faint ringing, and the girl in black ran through a door out of sight.

"In another hour," Madeira said softly, "she will be watching the curtain go up at the Forty-fourth Street Theater and—"

"The Shubert," Hyer corrected, "with a fat Major—"

"He'll only be a young Lieutenant, and he—"

"Want to bet?" Hyer asked.

"How can we settle it?"

"Go to the Forty-fourth Street Theater and catch the first two acts," Hyer said promptly. "Then drift over to the Shubert for a look-in at the end—"

"And then find the rowdiest and noisiest night club in town—"

"And ring doorbells all the way home."

Madeira laughed. "Shall we?"

"Why not?"

"If we could only take Angelica—"

"She's in bed every night at eight-thirty!" Hyer was shocked. "What kind of influence are you going to be in this—?" He stood up. "Now if you'll run along out of a gentleman's bedroom, Miss Thayer, he'll put on a tie and make himself decent for dinner."

An instant after she had left, Madeira thrust her head around the door. "Henry, I know a South American game that beats shooting craps. Want me to give Angelica a les—?" She ducked as Hyer threw a slipper.

17

ANGELICA, Madeira, and Hyer had just finished dinner but were still sitting at the table which Jonah had arranged at one of the open windows.

Madeira said, "Listen."

Across the quiet dripping gardens from another open window came a radio voice: ". . . How, who was arrested this morning in a rooming house in the Sixties on suspicion of murder, spent four hours in the Highbridge jail before being released. Meanwhile his picture had been published in metropolitan papers. The picture was recognized by Silas How, millionaire sportsman, as that of a long-lost favorite nephew. So Robert How, who was penniless and without a job when he got up this morning—who was a murder suspect at noon—is tonight established at his uncle's palatial Long Island estate for an indefinite visit. This summary of the news has come to you through the—" The radio was turned off.

Hyer said, "The American way. You can't match it."

"Boss," Jonah called from the door at the front of the room, "Mist' Cordero to see you."

Madeira stood up quickly. "Would you mind, Henry—? I mean—I think I'll sit this one out."

"You come help me," Angelica said eagerly. "I write a letter. To my brother in Montevideo, I write a letter." Then quickly to Hyer, "I tell him nothing, Tío Hank, about—what we discuss this morning, *tu sabes?*"

"That's good, honey." But there was a sudden uneasiness in his eyes. "Just as well nót to count chickens."

Madeira lingered a moment after Angelica had run upstairs. "Mind awfully?"

"Me? Mind?"

"Pedro can be difficult. I imagine he's furious—at our not waiting for him in Highbridge, I mean."

Hyer said, "Oh, that. Do you think I ought to apologize?"

"The odd part," Madeira confessed, "is that I completely forgot about Pedro. Did you, Henry?"

"No," Hyer said, "No—I didn't forget about him."

"Tell Pedro I'll see him tomorrow, Henry."

"Why?"

Madeira laughed. "Don't let him stay forever. You've got a date tonight, remember."

There was nothing forbidding about Cordero when Jonah ushered him in. The man's buoyant animal spirits were untouched, his black eyes lively as ever, his laughter as full and resonant. "So you and Madeira made your escape," he said cheerfully. "When I got back, the place was like a tomb."

"Not quite like a tomb," Hyer corrected. "What happened to Molloy and Della?"

Cordero grew serious. He sat down and took out a cigar. "In a way, I'm afraid I failed you, Hyer."

"Oh, I wouldn't say that."

Cordero looked up quickly. "But, you see—"

"Molloy and Doudy got away from you? Is that it?"

Cordero's vibrant self-possession faltered. "How did you know?"

Hyer waved his hand. "I didn't. It was a possibility."

Cordero, himself again, laughed. "Leaping at conclusions again, eh? Well— By the way, where is Madeira?"

"She had a headache. She says we'll all get together tomorrow."

Color flowed up from Cordero's ruddy beard to his temples. "We'll . . . *all* get together?"

"If you'd rather not, we can put it off."

Cordero studied Hyer. "A bit on edge, aren't you, amigo?"

"Something gave me a pain in the neck," Hyer said shortly. "What about Della and Molloy?"

Cordero lighted his cigar. "Odd thing. We hadn't gone more than a block or so when Molloy acted sick. So I stopped. He jumped out. Miss Doudy was right behind him. But do you know what the beggar did? Ran off between two houses like a madman—the Doudy woman right at his heels calling to him."

"And you couldn't catch them?"

Cordero grimaced and bent forward to rub his right shin. "There was a damned croquet court between those two houses." He shook his head and his white teeth showed. "When I picked myself up, I was out of the running. Looked as if I might have crawled down a coalhole. But I went on to Molloy's to see if he got home safely. Quite paralyzed the doorman, too, the state I was in. I waited outside the apartment house."

"Did Molloy get there?"

"Eventually. Twenty minutes later, perhaps. He and the Doudy woman came in a cab. She went in with him. So, since I had fulfilled my trust, I went back—and found you and Madeira gone. On the way here I stopped at home and cleaned up. I was a sight." Cordero laughed heartily.

"Well," Hyer said, "pretty soon the long arm of the law will be reaching for Klim."

Cordero's laughter ended. He drew on his cigar and frowned. "I've been thinking it over, Hyer. I wonder whether it's the right thing, after all."

"It was your idea."

Cordero nodded. "So it was. But sometimes in the heat of a situation—"

"Anyway," Hyer said firmly, "I made a deal with Lieutenant Cassius. If he hadn't kept his word, I might feel differently now. But he surprised me. Now it's up to me to surprise him."

"To surprise him?"

"I promised Cassius a confession," Hyer said bluntly. "In fact, I think I even set a deadline."

Cordero considered the ash on his cigar. "And, of course . . . Hen-ry," ironically, "being a man of your word—"

"Being a man of my word," Hyer said in a brittle voice, "yes, go on."

The doorbell rang.

In a moment Jonah's voice sounded. "Mist' Braun to see you, boss."

Cordero said, "Ah, the elusive Mr. Braun."

Into the microphone below the desk, Hyer said, "Bring him up, Jonah." He looked at Cordero, said, "All right. I'm waiting. Being a man of my word—"

"Need I finish?" Cordero asked. Then with sudden interest he looked toward the hall. "So I am at last to see our Mr. Braun, the bearer of tidings, who set the whole train of—"

Puffing, Jonah came to the door. "Mist' Albert Braun," he announced, and creased his bulging white coat in a bow.

Hyer said, "Come in, Braun. Cordero's getting ready to frame Klim and we may need your help."

Braun's squarish florid face had been set in lines of truculence as he walked briskly into the room. Now it changed abruptly, like a rigid polygon gone limp.

Cordero said sharply, "I say, Hyer, there's no point in being so—"

"Won't you sit down, Mr. Braun?"

Braun sat down. He raised one blunt-fingered hand and smoothed his thinning hair away from its plumb-line part.

"Wouldn't you pick Klim, Braun, as the logical candidate for framing?" Hyer asked.

"If this is another one of your practical jokes," Braun said angrily, "you can—"

"Or how about Braun himself?" Hyer asked Cordero brightly.

Braun stood up. "If you two think you can—" He was trembling.

"Braun knew where Reed was last night," Hyer continued thoughtfully. "Braun will say Reed didn't have the watch on him after he was killed. Braun—"

"*How* did I know where he was?"

"Because Klim told you. Because you took Reed to Highbridge in your car," Hyer answered. "He told you he had a date there and offered to give you the watch if you'd drive him up to a certain house, leave him, and then come back and pick him up about one-thirty or so."

"That's libelous. I'll have you—" Braun stopped, his fury cooled abruptly. "If I had killed him, then why would I have gone back there to pick him up when—?"

Hyer nodded at Cordero. "See? In many ways, Braun might make a better victim than Klim. He thinks fast.

He'd save the District Attorney a lot of questions on the stand."

Crimson, Braun strode to Hyer and seized his arm. "If you keep this up, perhaps I'll tell what I *do* know!" He looked swiftly at Cordero.

"Yes?" Cordero asked. "*What* do you know?"

"I know whose room Reed Molloy was killed in."

Cordero's broad shoulders swelled. He too rose from his chair. "Then you'd best forget it."

Hyer said, "I don't know. It'll help make him an interesting witness—if his lawyer's brash enough to put him on the stand. And then, of course, there's the motive to consider. If we use Braun, we'll have a ready-made motive and not have to do so much basting and fitting."

Braun laughed. He turned, walked away from the two men, and sat again.

Cordero asked curiously, "What motive?"

"Braun was afraid Reed might tell you how the two of them tried to cross you up, Cordero."

"Tell *me* how—?" Red flowed once more from under the thicket of Cordero's beard. "Look here, Hyer, what gives you the notion that I have anything to do with Braun?"

"The fact," Hyer said cheerfully, "that it didn't occur to you until now to ask that question."

"Nonsense."

"And the fact that Angelica found an envelope you'd dropped when you pulled your gloves out of your overcoat pocket yesterday evening."

Cordero's black eyes grew amused. "And the little devil read the letter, I suppose?" he asked casually.

Hyer was shocked. "*Angelica?*" (But he could see now that Cordero's amusement was edged with anger, and he regretted bitterly having brought Angelica into the melee.) Pain surged into Hyer's damaged tendons, and his fury at himself overflowed in a sudden acid impatience at the game they were playing.

"Braun works for you, Cordero," he said irascibly. "I didn't need a letter to tell me that. Last night I asked myself why Braun should be so anxious to advise me against taking a commission from you—when he himself had first gone to Madeira with the story of her father's death. By the way, Braun," he broke in and the corners of his nostrils flexed, "Madeira owes you something for that lie about her father having been . . . murdered. That was like breaking a child's arms to give it castor oil."

He walked to Braun, timing his own momentum and the arc of his blow with such nicety that he caught the other man squarely on the hinge of his jaw as Braun struggled to get out of the deep green chair. Man and chair went over with the deliberate finality of a slow-motion film.

Hyer, breathing rapidly, turned to face Cordero.

Cordero nodded. "I had been remembering that, myself. *Gracias*, amigo."

18

HYER sat on the corner of the desk, ignoring Braun, who was righting the chair. "John Thayer," he said to Cordero, "was bringing you some information from South America. Reed Molloy was following him, trying to get that information for somebody else. Who? Obviously for the johnny who'd hired Reed. And who had hired Reed?"

Hyer looked at Braun, now sullen in his chair. "You wanted Thayer's report so you could double-cross your employer, who was Señor Pedro Cordero. You thought Thayer might have put the report in his watch when he knew he was going to die. That's why you were so anxious to get the watch, isn't it? That's why you made up the story about his smuggling diamonds in the watch.

"Then when you thought the watch wasn't going to be found after Reed died, you fixed up a substitute and brought it to me to give to Madeira, hoping I'd lose interest. You knew there was a chance I might get too warm and show you up to Cordero. That," Hyer added in disgust, "was pretty dumb, incidentally."

Cordero glared at Braun. "Is all this true, Albert?"

"You won't take his word against mine?" Braun demanded.

Cordero's black eyes glittered. "But you admit you knew where Reed Molloy was last night—and yet you said nothing to me. But you knew I wanted to get the watch for Madeira."

"I admit nothing," Braun shouted. "What is this, a court?"

"That's right," Hyer agreed. "A kangaroo court. And now we'll have Exhibit A." He unlocked a drawer and drew out a rolled dustcloth. The cloth he opened on the desk. Shining brightly under the bronze-shaded lamp lay the revolver he had picked up under Madeira's window the night before.

Braun grasped the arms of his chair. Even the swelling bruise on the side of his jaw seemed to pale. "Where did you get that?"

"At the spot where Reed was killed."

"It was empty," Braun protested. "It couldn't—" He swallowed. He looked swiftly from Hyer to Cordero.

"Then it is true," Cordero said slowly, "that after

working for me honestly for twelve years, you were trying to get John Thayer's report . . . for yourself?"

Hyer swung the revolver gently from its trigger guard.

Braun nodded dazedly in time to Hyer's finger.

Cordero sat down. "The tragic part," he said softly, "is that John Thayer was carrying no report. If he *had* found the tin deposits, he was to have cabled me that the rumors were false. If he found nothing, he was to cable nothing. He had no report you could possibly have used, Albert."

The room was quiet for a moment. Hyer put the revolver down on the desk.

"Braun," Hyer said slowly, "you're a lot luckier than you've any right to be. Twenty-four hours ago this gun could have given you a neat handicap on the last mile. If I hadn't been the world's prize idiot right then—if I hadn't had an insane suspicion that . . . somebody *else* had dropped this—"

"Who?" Cordero asked.

Hyer said, "Never mind. I'll be the rest of my life living it down. At that, though, maybe it's just as well. If the police *had* found this gun—" His mouth tightened. "Don't forget, Cordero, that Squarehead here is anxious to remember whose room it was. No," decisively, "we've only one way to play it, Cordero."

"Only one way to—?"

"Klim," Hyer said.

Cordero thrust the back of his hand under his red beard, curling it up bushily across his mouth.

"Braun's testimony," Hyer continued, "will probably be all we'll need. Notice how it fits into the picture you helped me work out. Klim knew Reed had the watch. He found out last night that I'd give him two hundred and fifty dollars for it, and he went straight to the hotel to see Reed. But Reed had gone out with Braun. We'll say Klim had already told Braun where Reed was, of course."

Cordero glared at Braun.

"So Klim—we'll say—was afraid Braun would get the watch from Reed before *he* could. He was determined to cut Braun out, so he went up to Highbridge as fast as he could—"

"Wait," Cordero said, the word coming muffled through his upthrust beard. "How did Reed know where to find Madeira?"

"We'll say Klim told him. Nobody can dispute it now."

"And how did Klim know where she was?"

"I've worked that out," Hyer answered. "Braun had him watching Decker Molloy's apartment house. Has Klim told us everything he saw there? No. All right, we'll make up a story. We'll *say* Klim saw Reed—whom he was watching for—*with Molloy*. We'll give Klim a terrific curiosity. When he had put Reed up in the hotel here in New York Saturday, we'll say he went back just to see what was happening in Highbridge.

"We'll say he caught Decker Molloy going to the Doudy house. That turned his attention to the Doudy house. He knew about Madeira from the picture in the

watch. So—we'll say—he spent some time watching the
house and saw Madeira. That explains how he knew
where to go last night to look for Reed."

Hyer struck the desk suddenly. "By the way, this
afternoon the police got a tip that the room was a girl's
room when Reed was murdered. We'll tie that to Klim,
too."

Cordero's hand was still buried under the point of his
chin. The diamond winked through the roughened
beard. "But," he said slowly, "that makes Klim know
. . . too much."

"It's our story," Hyer snapped. "Not his. We'll say
he saw Reed get out of Braun's car last night. He crept
up behind Reed at the window. Reed stepped back and
discovered him. Klim— We'll say Klim caught him
around the throat and broke his neck. Maybe he didn't
mean to kill him. He just wanted the watch. But then
people started going past from the movie and he found
he'd killed Reed. So, we'll say—just as you suggested
this evening—he tumbled Reed into the room, climbed
in after him, pulled down the window, and locked it."

Hyer looked hard at Cordero. "Then—as you said—
it was possible that Klim found a trunk in the closet—a
trunk full of a young actor's things. Let's say Klim
found the trunk, broke it open, and scattered the things
around for a red herring. Then he sneaked out the front
door—with the watch he'd taken out of Reed's pocket—
and came back to New York. How about it?" Hyer
asked Cordero.

Cordero frowned and looked away.

"This morning," Hyer continued persuasively, "we'll say that Klim went to Reed's hotel room and put the watch on the bureau. They all use skeleton keys in that hotel anyway. Then he came to get me. He and I found the watch. Q.E.D."

Cordero withdrew his hand and stroked his beard back into place rapidly. "Hyer, I don't— But what about the gun?"

"No trouble at all. It—"

"It was in the glove compartment of my car," Braun broke in. "I swear I didn't know Reed had taken it out. I only missed it a little while ago—as I was on my way here. I swear I didn't know—"

"That's it," Hyer said to Cordero. "Reed took Braun's revolver out of the glove compartment as he rode up to Highbridge with Braun last night. He was holding it when Klim jumped him. He dropped it. And finally," Hyer said with emphasis, "we've got Mr. Braun himself to put the finishing touch on it for us."

Cordero's bright black eyes sought Braun, who sat tensely grasping the arms of his chair.

"Braun," Hyer said, "went back to Abbey Street to get Reed. He's admitted it to us. He waited a little where he could watch the house—we'll say. We'll say— and *he'll* say—he saw Klim come out. Well? What more do we need?"

Braun squirmed. "I won't perjure myself."

Hyer idly pushed the revolver in a half-circle with his fingernail. "Won't you?"

Braun wet his lips.

"What about the hotel clerk?" Cordero demanded abruptly. "He can give Klim an alibi." When Hyer hesitated for the first time, Cordero added emphatically, "I don't like that, Hyer. Not," quickly, "that I like any of it, of course. But it seems to me we're overlooking the most important thing. The hotel clerk—"

"One man's word against a chain of evidence," Hyer scoffed.

"Look here," Cordero burst out, "this whole thing—"

The telephone rang.

The three waited.

It rang again.

From the speaker came Jonah's voice. "Mist' Klim for you, boss."

Cordero's hand leaped up to ruffle his beard.

Braun moved as if to get up. He sat back. He was white.

Hyer looked from one to the other. Braun dropped his glance quickly. Cordero was frowning, and there was a struggle in his intent black eyes.

"Well?" Hyer asked softly.

Neither of his guests moved.

Hyer reached for the telephone.

"*No*," Cordero said. "*No, Hyer!*"

Hyer's hand halted. "Madeira, then?"

Cordero grasped his temples, grinding the heels of his hands into his eyes. He muttered something.

"We can't fool ourselves any longer," Hyer said softly.

"Boss," Jonah called, "you hear me?"

Cordero's hands slid down his cheeks, cupped his luxuriant beard in a V. During the moment his eyes had been hidden, they had suffered a change. The bright life had left them. They were haggard—and they gave assent.

Hyer said, "Hello! . . . Oh, hello, Klim. . . . That's right, I came down from Highbridge a long time ago. . . . Yes, right after Cordero and Molloy left. . . . You lost 'em? . . . Oh, you didn't have a cab right then? . . . No, it's all right. I know what happened, anyway. . . . Where are you now? . . . How long will it take you to get back to the city? . . . All right, suppose you come here to my house. I've got—something else for you to do. . . . Yes, I'll wait. . . . All right. . . . All right."

He put the phone down as carefully as though it were made of glass.

In the silent room Braun's breathing was loud and rapid.

Hyer, his eyes holding Cordero's, leaned down to touch the speaker switch.

In a moment, Jonah's voice came briskly from the speaker. "Yes, boss?"

"Get me Lieutenant Cassius in Highbridge, Jonah," Hyer said. There was something almost gentle in his tone.

Cordero stood up, Braun following suit like a shadow.

"Wouldn't it be better," Cordero asked, "if Braun and I weren't here when—? Well, wouldn't it be better?"

Hyer nodded. He said, "Much better, gentlemen.

Much . . . better." The lines of strain that deepened beside his mouth were still there when he heard the front door close, heard one car start and an instant later another.

Steps, descending from the floor above, approached.

In one continuous movement, Hyer swung himself off the desk, whipped the revolver into its cloth, dropped the rolled cloth into the drawer, and was turning—his bland, good-natured self once more—to the door as Madeira tapped and opened it.

"Henry," she asked, "does Pedro know . . . yet?"

"Know what, Madeira?"

Madeira had been coming toward him eagerly. She stopped. She flushed. "Never mind. It was a silly thing to ask." She drew a breath and walked to one of the windows. She opened the drapes and looked down into Bank Street.

The room was silent.

When Hyer stood at her side, Madeira said softly, "Angelica wrote a sweet letter to her brother."

"Does Pedro know what?" Hyer asked.

"She told her brother he might have a surprise in store for him."

Hyer caught the tip of her nose with his crooked finger and drew her face toward him. "Know what, Madeira?"

She tried to turn away.

"Know what?" Hyer murmured.

"Pedro," she whispered, "is a very . . . possessive guy, Henry. Or hadn't you noticed?"

Hyer grinned at her. "There's something somewhere about the chap with that mote in his eye." He waited. "Does Pedro know . . . what?"

Her mouth twisted. "*Pero—verdad—no hablo las palabras inglesas, Enrique mío, para* . . . and anyway it would sound much better in Spanish. Shall we wait until Angelica comes back to help me tell you?"

Hyer's eyes grew suddenly quiet. "Wait until Angelica comes *back*, Madeira?"

"She went out to post her letter. Just to the corner."

"How long ago?" Hyer demanded.

"Only a minute. She ran down just before I came in here to— Henry, you're trembling!"

Hyer patted her shoulder. "I'll just run down and meet her." From the door he said, "You wait here—so we can all have that Spanish lesson." He smiled, but the smile was too brittle.

"Henry." Madeira started toward him.

"We'll be right up!" Hyer called.

He ran down the stairs three at a time. "God!" . . . he pleaded, "God!" . . . He stumbled at the last step, steadied himself, stood an instant staring blindly at the street door, seized the knob, and ran out.

19

AT twelve-thirty that night, Schultz of the fingerprint detail stopped his muddy roadster in Bank Street three doors from Hyer's house. The space in front of him was solidly lined with cars. Two were white-topped police coupés, their radio sets growling in unison. Two others were prowl-cars of the detective division. Beyond these were three taxicabs, a limousine, and a newspaper truck.

Schultz got out of the muddy roadster wearily and plodded past the official fleet. He nodded to the men sitting in the cars. "Hi, Mac. . . . 'Lo, Bert. . . . Evening, Inspector." He mounted the steps to Hyer's stoop, nodded at two plain-clothesmen sitting on the railing, and went in the open door.

In the small sitting room at his left, two city detectives were talking in low voices. A cab-driver with a harelip and a broken nose came down the stairs, jerking his cap into place and muttering.

"Any news yet, Snuff?" Schultz asked.

"Think thunh plance'd be full of comps sittin' aroun' on thunhr cans if thunhr was?" Snuff jerked viciously at his cap. He glared at Schultz. "Linke to genht *my* hand on thunh sonofunhbinch . . ." He went out, muttering nasally.

Schultz plodded up the stairs, nodded to a young detective who met him running down, and then stood aside on the landing to let Jonah sidle past balancing an empty tray.

Jonah said, "Evenin', Mist' Schultz. Go right in like nothin' had—" He stopped, swallowed.

"Hank in there?"

"Nossuh." Jonah swallowed again. "Ain' been back since jus' aft' he try to phone you."

Schultz said gruffly, "I was up in the country."

"Ain' *no*body know whe'at he is." Jonah's triple chins quivered. Then, aware of his stewardship, he asked politely, "You want bourbon same as always, Mist'—?"

"Hell with bourbon," Schultz growled. He plodded on up and across the hall.

The long room was full of smoke and the murmur of men talking.

As Schultz entered, the telephone rang.

Instantly the voices were silent.

A young patrolman standing near the desk reached
for the telephone.

But Madeira Thayer, sitting behind the desk, drew the
instrument toward her swiftly, her dark eyes challeng-
ing. She looked toward the window at her right.
"Ready?" she asked.

The telephone under her hand rang again.

Another patrolman standing at the open window
called guardedly down to the street, "All right, Bert."

Through the hush, those in the room could hear a
man outside say, "Calling WPDP, calling WP— Mac,
trace another call into Chelsea 9-1102. Rush it."

Again the phone rang.

Madeira was white. She said, "I don't dare wait too
long."

"Give 'em one more," a long-faced official with a
gold badge advised. "Then be ready to keep whoever
it is talking, miss."

The phone rang a fourth time.

The man with the gold badge nodded.

Madeira picked up the telephone. "Hello! . . ." She
gave a start. "Oh, hello, Pedro. . . ." Strain drew the
corners of her mouth taut as she glanced at the man in
the window.

Madeira said, "Why, no, Pedro, he's not—" stopped
as a dozen men stepped toward her, gesturing fiercely.
"Yes, I hear him now, Pedro," she said swiftly, her
cheeks flaming. "Just a minute. . . . What? No, Klim
didn't come. . . . Yes, he telephoned again. . . . Oh,
just a little while ago. He said he saw a police car in

front and was afraid to come in. . . . A trap?" Madeira
was white again. "Yes, I think he suspected it was a
trap. I tried to tell him— . . . Henry? Why, in just a
minute. He's coming up the— Pedro— *Pedro!*"

The young patrolman and the man with the gold
badge both reached for the telephone. Gold Badge
jerked it from Madeira's hand. He listened, shook his
head. "Hung up. Next time, miss," he said sternly, "let
somebody else."

Madeira rose. Her face was scarlet. She came from
behind the desk and walked down the long room.

A man squatting on his heels before the doll's house
looked over his shoulder, saw the anguish in the girl's
face. "That's O.K., miss," he said softly. "It was somebody you knew, anyway. Don't let Horseface bother
you."

Madeira stood at one of the garden windows, clutching the drapes, trembling. The inner square of the block
was quiet, dark, rain-scented. At irregular intervals drops
fell from the ailanthus tree to the roof of Angelica's
playhouse. A drugget of light lay across the grass from
a window below, and as Madeira watched, the Burke
tomcat stalked silently through it and vanished.

At her shoulder a gruff voice said, "You're Miss
Thayer, I guess, miss."

Madeira turned her head. She bit her lip and nodded
at the short bullet-headed man beside her.

"My name's Schultz, miss. Hank left a message I was
to contact you if I missed him." He hesitated, added
awkwardly, "I was up in the country."

One corner of Madeira's lips lifted in a smile. She said, "It was good of you to come, Mr. Schultz. Henry wanted you."

"Where's he at now, miss?"

Strain drew at her mouth again. "He went out with Sergeant Tooley. About two hours ago."

"Sixth Precinct," Schultz murmured absently. "They have anything to go on, you know, miss?"

"There was a taxicab stolen from the corner just about— A little before nine."

"Always being careless, hackies," Schultz observed. "Any news about it yet?"

Madeira shook her head.

"You here when it happened, miss?"

Madeira turned abruptly and looked hard at the sleeping gardens. "Yes . . . I was here."

Presently Schultz said, "I don't suppose there's anything for me to work on yet. Any note or anything?"

"No."

They stood for a time without further talk. Behind them the long room was murmurous. In the house across the darkened gardens, a light came on. The girl in the black evening dress came in, closed the door, leaned against it for an instant, and then threw herself on the bed, her face in her arms.

Madeira turned from the window.

"If you want to tell me about—" Schultz began. "Being you were here when—"

"Don't, Schultz."

The bullet-headed man looked at her, his eyes not unkindly. "You a relative of Angelica's by any chance, miss?"

Madeira clenched her hands and walked toward the bedroom door. She stopped, stood rigid a moment, and came back. She said, "Angelica wrote a letter. She went out to mail it at the corner. She didn't come back. It was a little before nine."

Schultz considered this. "A little before nine? Up later'n usual, then, wasn't she?"

Madeira's breath caught. There was a choking of laughter in her throat. "You even know . . . Angelica's bedtime?"

"Sure, miss."

"But how could— You're Schultz," Madeira said slowly. "You're a policeman, a fingerprint expert."

"Anybody't knew Hank Hyer, miss, knew Angelica— knew all about Angelica. Why, hear Hank talk you'd think the sun and moon was only put up for Angelica's benefit." He looked at Madeira curiously. "Why you suppose all these guys—pardon me, miss—these men are here?"

"There were twelve taxi-drivers," Madeira said unsteadily.

Schultz nodded. "Be coming all night prolly—as news gets around. If this was the West, miss, you'd see the biggest posse ever made up." He regarded the grim-faced men in the room. "Sometimes," he said slowly, "seems like city life's a handicap some ways."

Madeira shook her head. "All of these men—the cab-drivers, the police—are friends of Henry's?"

"Friends of Hank's?" Schultz echoed in mild surprise. "See that pair there leaning on the piano? One of 'em— the thin one keeps hunching his coat collar—he's Mal Range. Writes this column in the *Examiner*, you know? Hank beat the daylights outta Mal one time for printing something about some girl. She was a redhead. Hank always went for redheads."

"Tell me more, Schultz."

"The one with Mal, that's Al Jocelyn. He's a big lawyer. Hank saved his wife from the chair, I guess. Before she was Mrs. Jocelyn, that was. Come to think of it, she's got red hair, too."

"Has she?"

Schultz glanced at Madeira in sudden confusion. "Of course, there been brunettes—"

"Of course. In droves."

Schultz's confusion increased. "I wouldn't say that exactly, miss."

"Pursuing him, the hussies."

"Anyway," Schultz said quickly, "you see them four up there around the desk? All first-grade detectives. Hear 'em talk, you'd think they'd cut Hank's heart out for all the tricks he's played on 'em one time or another. Well, you see that doll's house there?"

Madeira closed her eyes. She nodded.

"Cost six hundred dollars, that doll's house. Them four dicks give it to Angelica for Christmas."

Madeira bit her lip.

"The one standing there talking down to the street," Schultz continued, "he's Inspector F. X. Turner. One

time when F. X. was only just a captain, he had trouble
with Hank Hyer over a client of Hank's. Once Hank
takes a client, miss, he'll fight through hell and all for
'em."

Madeira said, "Go on, Schultz."

"Anyway, F. X. there, he arrested Hank in the lobby
of the St. Julian that time." Schultz chuckled. "Hank
got to a phone and called police headquarters, told 'em
there was a explosion and a fire at the St. Julian, and
in three minutes every riot car in Manhattan come
screamin' up—and Hank walked out a side door in all
the confusion. F. X. swore he'd kill 'im."

"And yet they all—like Henry."

"*Like* Hank? Look," Schultz said, "you ever see a
play name of *What Price Glory?*, miss? Well, if every
cop in New York was Captain Flagg, there'd be only
one Sergeant Quirt and I guess you know what his
name'd be." Schultz was thoughtful a moment. "Do you
know," he said, interested, "if the guy wrote that play
had only put Angelica—"

In the street outside there were voices and running
footsteps. The room stirred. Men set down their drinks,
turned, got up from chairs.

Feet ran up the stairs, across the hall.

Henry Hyer came into the room, hatless, his hair
wind-whipped, a streak of dirt across one temple. He
glanced about, strode toward Madeira, who was running
to meet him in the middle of the room.

A man coughed. There was a flurry of awkward conversation which ceased a moment later as Hyer, his

arm about Madeira, went on down the room and through the door at the right.

Just as Hyer and Madeira disappeared, Lieutenant Cassius came in from the hall. His seamed sachem face under the snowy hair was stolid.

A little later Schultz stood in the open bedroom door and coughed.

Hyer, sitting on the bed, his shoulders slumped forward, his hands hanging between his knees, glanced up. There was a harried, distracted look in his eyes.

Madeira, beside him, held out her hand for one of the two glasses Schultz carried, shook her head when he would have given her both. She said, "Here, Henry."

Hyer took the glass, drank absently. He said, "Hello, Schultz." His voice was lifeless. "Tried to get you." He put the glass on the floor.

"I was up in the country, Hank. I come as soon as I heard."

Range, the thin columnist, appeared in the doorway carrying two glasses. "Here, Hank." He handed one to Hyer, and his nervous hand leaped up to adjust his coat collar.

Hyer looked up. "Thanks, Mal." He took a sip of the highball, set it on the floor.

"They're doing all they can, Hank," Range said. He dropped a hand on Hyer's shoulder, turned, and went out, tugging at his collar.

Lieutenant Cassius came to the door. He looked impassively at Madeira. "Hyer," he said in his slow, official-report manner, "they say Klim called up here."

Hyer's haggard glance leaped to Madeira.

"Just a little while ago, Henry," Madeira said. "He saw a police car in front and didn't want to come in."

"We've got men at every corner in four blocks in case he comes back," Cassius said.

"Excuse me, Hank," the long-faced official with the gold badge said from the doorway, "but who would a guy named Pedro be?"

"Pedro Cordero," Madeira answered.

"Thanks, miss. Who would he be, Hank?"

Hyer was staring at him fixedly. "Did *he* call?"

"Miss Thayer here talked to him."

Hyer stood up.

"Pedro wanted to know whether Klim had come," Madeira said.

"Hank! Hank!" One of the four detectives who had stood at the desk ran into the bedroom. "They found the hack, Hank!"

"*Where?*"

"On River Parkway, just above the Norcross line."

"On the way to Highbridge!" Madeira cried.

Hyer's eyes were wild. He wet his lips. "Or—on—the way—back."

"Cassius!" someone called from the room. Someone else said, "He's in there."

The young patrolman ran to the doorway, said over Gold Badge's shoulder, "Highbridge just sent out a call for you to phone in, Lieutenant."

Hyer stumbled over Madeira's ankles and seized the extension telephone from the window ledge. His mouth

twitched. He said, "Police headquarters, Highbridge,"
handed the instrument to Cassius.

Jocelyn pushed through the knot of men in the doorway. He said, "Henry, I thought I'd come down in case
I could do anything."

Hyer, his frantic glance not leaving Cassius' face, murmured, "Thanks, Al."

"Hello!" Cassius said. "Cassius. . . . Yes, what about
him? . . . Where? . . . Did he admit—? . . . All right.
. . . All right." He put the phone down.

Hyer caught his arm.

"They found your left-handed seaman, Hyer," Cassius said.

Hyer's hand dropped. Bitter disappointment showed
in his drawn face. He turned away. Again his mouth
twitched.

"Well," Cassius asked, "aren't you interested?"

Hyer's eyes rested on Madeira. He drew a deep
breath. He said, "I'm interested."

"He's a deck officer on a boat in last Friday from
Rio." Admiration showed in Cassius' normally stolid
face. "It's just the way you said. He told them he—"

The phone rang.

Hyer wheeled and seized it. He said, "Hello! . . .
Oh, hello, Della. . . . He what?" Listening, Hyer said
rapidly to Cassius, "Molloy just shot himself."

Madeira cried, "No—no!" . . .

"Yes, Della," Hyer said. "Yes, Della. . . . No, I don't
blame you for not going back to—" He broke off, his

eyes lighting wildly. The phone fell with a clatter to the floor.

Hyer grasped Cassius' arm, hurtled through the group in the doorway, drawing the white-haired Lieutenant after him. Madeira, flying down the stairs, caught up with them at the sidewalk.

"But my driver went to get a sandwich," Cassius was saying. "I'm no good at night driving. My eyes—"

Madeira said, "I'll drive."

Hyer caught her hand. The three of them ran toward a sedan parked behind Schultz's muddy roadster.

20

CASSIUS said slowly, "I wonder why Molloy did it."

They were speeding along the parkway now, the city far behind them, suburban meadows drowsing on either side. Madeira glanced at Hyer, looked past him quickly at the Lieutenant, and then back at the road.

Hyer sat rigidly erect, one hand braced on the instrument panel, his forefinger ready at a button controlling the car's siren. His lips were moving.

"Any idea why he'd do a thing like that, Hyer?" Cassius asked.

Madeira said, "The dead man was his brother."

Cassius gave a start. One hand lifted automatically to cross himself. "Decker Molloy's brother?"

Hyer said, "Faster. For God's sake . . ."

"And Molloy stood there last night," Cassius murmured, "looked down at the poor guy—and didn't turn a hair."

After a time Hyer said wearily, "He turned. Only it was inside."

Cassius was thoughtful. "Then that's what was wrong with him this afternoon?"

"Faster!" Hyer said to Madeira.

"He looked like a crazy man," Cassius said.

"He was one."

Madeira laid her hands on Hyer's. "Was that why you wanted Della to stay with him, Henry?"

"Somebody had to." Hyer's shoulders jerked. "Only it didn't work." He struck the instrument panel with his fist. "Faster!"

Presently Cassius said, "I want to get this straight." He looked at Hyer quickly. "That is, if you don't mind talking."

"No." Hyer's finger jabbed at the siren button as a car turned into the parkway ahead of them. The car shied away as they wailed past.

"Maybe," Cassius said gruffly, "it'll help keep your mind off the kid."

Madeira put her hand over Hyer's quickly.

"You tell me," Cassius continued slowly, "that the guy who killed this Reed Mallory—or Reed *Molloy*, if what you say is true—is named Klim and—"

"But, Henry—"

The siren screamed, deafening them.

"Eben Klim," Hyer said harshly to Cassius. "Yes, the one you're trying to pick up."

Madeira bit her lip.

"Why did he do it?" Cassius asked. "Do you know?"

Hyer said, "Klim and Reed were on a ship that went down. They spent three weeks on a raft together."

"That's why he looked the way he did last night, Mallory—I mean Molloy?" Cassius nodded. "Of course we knew he'd been in a hospital. We didn't know why."

"He and Klim were picked up at sea. Then Reed ran out on Klim. He had something Klim thought he deserved a share in."

Madeira drew a quick breath. Hyer's hand fell from the button to her knee.

"You mean Reed double-crossed this Klim?" Cassius asked. "So that's the way it was."

"Klim followed Reed from Charleston," Hyer said. "He saw him leave Molloy's apartment house in Highbridge and followed him to New York. He persuaded Reed to put up at a fifty-cent hotel. Reed had had a quarrel with his brother by that time."

Again the siren screamed and died. "Klim's got a fanatical kind of curiosity," Hyer continued. "He came back up here to Highbridge and watched for Reed's brother. He'd seen them together, but didn't know they were brothers. He followed Molloy to Della Doudy's— he'd had experience shadowing people."

Cassius said, "Um, Della Doudy's. The way she went home with Molloy this afternoon—well, you'd think there might have been something between them."

Hyer's nostrils quivered. He said, "Something, yes."

After a moment Cassius said, "We were talking about Klim."

"Oh, yes. Well, last night Klim followed Reed up to Highbridge from New York. Reed went to Della Doudy's house—"

"His brother was there then, maybe?"

Hyer nodded, "Molloy was there. Reed started to climb in a window. Klim sneaked up on him and there was a fight. People came out of the theater just then, and when Klim found he'd killed Reed, he pushed him through the window and climbed in himself."

"There in that room where we found him, you mean?"

Hyer nodded.

Madeira made a sound.

"Oh," Cassius said, "then Klim's the one scattered those clothes around?"

"I wouldn't put it past him," Hyer answered shortly. Again his hand dropped warningly on Madeira's knee.

"Found the trunk in the closet, I suppose," Cassius hazarded. "Kind of a stupid thing to do, if you ask me."

Hyer's finger leaped to the siren button.

"But," Cassius said when the siren had run down, "what made Della Doudy tell her story about a roomer that never existed?"

"She thought she was protecting Molloy," Hyer said promptly. "If you want to hold that against her, you can, but she's a woman."

"Obstructing justice."

"What do you care, as long as you get your confession?"

Cassius shook his head. "People can't obstruct justice, Hyer."

In a moment Hyer said, "So you're going to try to make things hard for Della?"

"She'll have some explaining to do," Cassius predicted.

"To whom?"

"What do you mean?"

Hyer said persuasively, "Why go to all the trouble of arresting Della, Lieutenant, when the most it can get you is another political feud or two?"

Cassius shook his head. "I don't—"

"Will the courthouse gang let anybody whip up a scandal at Molloy's expense?" Hyer looked at Cassius' impassive Indian profile. "You'll be accused of picking on Molloy because he's dead. They'll make a martyr out of him. They'll call you a coward. You won't have a chance, Lieutenant. Even Molloy's enemies will look cross-eyed at you. Nobody likes a man who tries to make political capital out of a suicide."

Cassius stared at a railroad embankment lifting swiftly at their right.

"How about it?" Hyer asked. "If you let Della alone, nobody else is going to bother her. If you get your confession—"

"If I get it."

"You'll get it," Hyer promised.

After a long time, Cassius said, "All right, then. We'll forget Della."

They raced into the outskirts of Highbridge. The siren wailed. Hyer leaned forward, the tendons at his throat stiffening.

Presently he lifted his finger from the button, motioned to Madeira to slow down. In a moment he said, "Turn here," his voice queer. Then, "Stop!" He switched off the lights.

They were in darkened Abbey Street a block from the ugly stone house. Beyond were the lights of the avenue. After their roaring flight, the silence was heavy, muffling.

"I'm going on ahead," Hyer said. "I'm going alone."

"Henry—"

"All night," Hyer continued furiously, "I've tried to think where—" The muscles in his jaw flexed. "I've tried to think where she might be. I think I know."

"Della's?" Madeira cried. "But why—?"

"Della made it clear to me she wasn't going back there—that the house would be empty. Remember," he asked Cassius, "I told you over the phone when I called you from here?"

"And you think the kidnapper knows the house will be empty?" Cassius asked.

"Let me out," Hyer commanded. He reached over Cassius, threw open the door.

Cassius stepped out. He caught Hyer's arm when Hyer leaped to the ground, said, "Take it easy."

Hyer struck the other man's hand away. He was panting. "If you try to go with me, I'll kill you. She's mine —mine."

"We'll wait for you," Cassius said. "We'll wait here."

Hyer thrust his fingers into his hair. He said, calmer now, "Sorry. Only if anything happens to that kid— If I had to think somebody else was to blame—"

"We'll wait, Hyer. Here, you'll need a flashlight." Cassius took one from a compartment and gave it to Hyer.

Madeira ran after Hyer, overtook him as he strode past the picket gate where they had taken shelter after they had escaped from the house. She said, "Henry," urgently.

Hyer stopped.

"Let me go with you, Henry." The request was humble.

"No."

"Do you really believe—what you told us?"

"I don't know, Madeira." Hyer's voice was suddenly listless.

"This isn't still part of—? Henry, you're not going to let them do that to Klim?" she asked passionately. "Hasn't there been enough tragedy without—Klim?"

Hyer drew her to him. "If I find what I think I'll find—*pray God I'll find*—then we'll clear Klim all up, Madeira." He kissed her, said roughly, "Now leave me alone."

He went on.

On the other side of the street, the stone house was an ugly dark shadow in the night. When he had passed it, when the corner of the theater had hidden it, Hyer crossed the pavement, stopped in the dark lee of the theater, and sought to control the pounding of his pulse.

He whispered, "Angelica . . . honey," and his throat constricted.

He walked along the wall of the theater until he came to the alley. His hand went to his pocket, to the other pocket. Under the night wind's touch, sweat was suddenly chill on his forehead. Not until this instant had he remembered that on returning home he had changed clothes. The key to the house was in the trousers which Jonah had carried away to the basement for sponging.

The hulk of the house loomed, silent, lifeless. Aware of the hopeless odds, Hyer felt the night surge about him—the night in whose ocean of blackness somewhere a little girl was waiting, terrified, trusting him because he had never before failed her.

Swiftly Hyer crossed the open space of the alley and ran to the house across the soundless sod. Moving more cautiously now, and avoiding the cement walk, he passed under the window where twenty-four hours earlier Reed Molloy had stood, and came eventually to the back of the house.

He waited, listened. A car hissed on the damp avenue. Then once more silence was like an uneasy tide drowning the house, stifling the breath in his lungs.

He crept forward past the shallow steps to the kitchen door, came to the far corner of the house. Here he waited again. His ears rang. His eyes were feverish, their lids like harsh abrasive.

Hyer went down on his knees and moved silently along the foundation of the house. He was now on the side away from the theater. Ten feet ahead of him was the cellar window which Madeira had found open when she climbed down from the room above. Automatically Hyer looked up.

As he approached the cellar window, the blood pounded in his throat. If his wild hypothesis were right, any least noise might bring disaster. Worse than disaster, for disaster was but an instant thing, and this might mean a lifetime of anguish. It came to Hyer, like something in the leisurely processes of a drowning man's mind, that never before in his crisis-strewn career had the future been anything but an empty frame in which certain things would happen and other things not happen—a frame as indifferent to the present as the rooms ahead of him are indifferent to a casual museum visitor.

But at this moment the future was terrifyingly real. Failure now would be no mere isolated incident to be written off and left behind him. Failure now would poison the rest of his days.

He came to the edge of the window, paused, holding his breath until a new ache paralyzed his throat. There was no sound. His hand trembling, he felt forward, slipped his fingers past the window frame. The sash was hinged at the top. It had been hooked open when he had been in the basement. Now it had fallen into place. Hyer's pent breath escaped.

With his fingers he pushed gently on the bottom of the sash. It held fast. He remembered the tinkle of glass he had heard through the grille in the living room. He hunched himself closer and felt along the lower edge of the sash. A pointed shard pricked him. The center pane was broken.

With the utmost care, he put his hand through the break and found the catch. Once more a thought came to him with the drowsy clarity of a drowning scene: under cover of the trumpeting thunder at dusk, a glass pane could have been smashed without being heard abovestairs.

He found the catch closed. Slowly he applied pressure until it turned. The hinged sash gave. An inch at a time, he raised it. Bracing himself against the frame, he reached in and felt for the hook which would hold the sash open. He was working boldly in front of the window now, gambling that the deep of the night was black enough not to silhouette him for an observer within.

He found the hook. The sash held open.

Hyer took off his shoes, felt muddy water flood through his socks. Then he sat at the edge of the sill, drew up his feet, and pivoted soundlessly. Turning, he put the heels of his hands flat on the sill, lifted himself on his rigid forearms, and let himself down, walking down the inner wall with his knees to keep the least scratch of cloth from sounding. His toes touched the solid floor and he stood erect breathing lightly.

Step by step he felt his way to the stairs. His fingers were on the invisible handrail when he stopped, stiffening like a man struck by high voltage.

The blood pounded behind his eyes.

He heard the sound again. A tiny stifled whimper.

He whirled, driven now by a maniac haste, felt his
way, guided by the faint whimper that was like a bayonet
thrust in his throat.

He came to a wooden partition, felt frenziedly for a
door, found a hasp with a wooden peg in it. The peg
scraped as he withdrew it, and at the sound the whim-
pering within stopped.

Hyer pushed the door open. "*Angelica,*" he whispered, "Angelica . . . honey."

A sob. "Tío Hank—"

The flashlight in Hyer's hand leaped alight.

Cowering under a shelf laden with jars was Angelica.
Her gray jumper was torn. There was a dark bruise
above one eye. She threw herself into Hyer's arms as
the flashlight, still burning, rolled across the floor.

Hyer held her, his throat jerking.

Angelica's hands moved convulsively over his face and
then her arms were about his neck, crushing his cheek
to hers.

"I know you come," she whispered, "but—it was—
long, *tío mío.*"

"Baby . . ."

She whispered, "I try to be brave so you won't need
be—*cómo se dice*—ashamed for me."

"Ashamed of . . . *you*, honey?"

She lifted her head from his shoulder, said at his ear,
"But once I weep. When—" She screamed.

As Hyer whirled, Angelica threw herself from him
to free him.

With a bellow of ancient atavistic blood lust, Hyer hurled himself at the figure that blocked the door.

Angelica screamed again. Then she scrambled to her feet, looked wildly around the room, caught up the flashlight in one hand and an empty bottle in the other, and flew to the fray.

On the cement floor at the foot of the stairs, Hyer was on his knees astride a struggling shape, his fists driving rhythmically and murderously into the face of Eben Klim.

"You were down here—" Hyer panted in time to his pistoning fists—"heard through the grille—what I said to Cassius—about the left-handed friend of yours—knew your number was up—mugged me when I came down here—"

"Tío Hank," Angelica cried.

Hyer held his next blow poised. "What?"

"*Must* you kill him—really?" Angelica asked anxiously. "He did not hurt me—so much."

Hyer groaned. The fist crashed into Klim's bleeding mouth.

Then Hyer sat back. "You weren't in Highbridge when you telephoned me at nine o'clock tonight, Klim. You were down in Greenwich Village, right around the corner from my house. I guessed it at the time."

"The corner by the mailbox," Angelica agreed. "He grab me like this." She clapped a small hand over her mouth and clutched her midriff. "He throw me in a taxicab." She looked suddenly abashed. "I guess I—*cómo se dice*—pass out, Tío Hank."

Hyer glared at the damaged Klim. "You saw the first police car come up to my house and that gave you your cue. The next time when you called and pretended you were down there—scared away by the police—you were really up here. Probably on your way back from getting rid of the cab."

After a moment, Angelica asked curiously, "How you know to come here to this place, Tío Hank?"

"He had to take you somewhere, baby. He's a stranger in New York, and a stranger with a little girl under his arm is under a pretty lively handicap. But he'd heard me tell a policeman over the phone that the—the Señorita who owns this house was going to be away for a while. He knew his way around downstairs here," Hyer added dryly.

He tried to get up, fell back with a groan.

"What's the matter?" Angelica cried.

Hyer rolled off the unconscious Klim, pulled himself up by the handrail, and sat on the bottom step of the stairs. He felt down his right leg, wincing. "Baby," he said in disgust, "I broke my ankle. You'll have to go get the Señorita Thayer, I guess."

Angelica swallowed. In a small voice she said, "Yes, Tío Hank." She hesitated. "But I have no money—and you must tell me where the train station is."

Hyer chuckled. "Come here."

For a moment he held her to him, his fingers playing hungrily through her straight black hair. "You'd do it, too, wouldn't you, honey?" he whispered.

"If you tell me to, Tío Hank."

Hyer said, "She's down the street, baby. Waiting for us. Here, I'll stand up and give you a boost to the window. Fine time," he grumbled, hoisting himself, "to break an ankle."

"I do not mind, Tío Hank," Angelica said hastily.

Hyer blinked. "*You* don't mind—you little sadist!"

"Of course," comfortably. "Some other time we go to Montevideo to see my brother, no?"

(

21

PROPPED up in bed, Hyer said, "That's right. It was from something you told me."

Pedro Cordero thrust the back of his hand under his chin and ruffled his beard. His black eyes glittered. "*Dios mío, qué hombre!*"

Angelica, sitting beside Hyer in the bed, tucked up her blue bathrobe sleeves and hugged her knees. "*Es un gran hombre, mi* Tío Hank."

Cordero laughed. He leaned forward and pinched a small toe. "*Estas muy feliz con él, querida?*"

Angelica nodded rapidly. Her eyes shone. "*Porqué le quiero.*"

"Secrets," Hyer grumbled, "are bad enough. Secrets in Spanish—"

"A very complimentary secret, Henry." Again Cordero laughed. "You have a way with women, amigo. But now, you were saying—"

"When we sat there in Della's curiosity shop yesterday evening," Hyer said, "you told me a long story about Carib ancestors. Remember?"

"Very well."

"Remember the yarn about the two who ordered the shipful of Indians to lie on their backs and push the deck up?"

Cordero nodded.

Angelica shivered with excitement.

"Right then," Hyer said, "I saw a picture. I saw a man lying in an iron bed, putting his feet against the rods at the bottom, and pushing them so they bent out. He would be a very tall man to get leverage enough. He would be a left-handed man because every time he got out of bed to pour himself a drink he sloshed a little liquor over his glass, and the liquor didn't run down on the washstand or to the left-of the washstand the way it would for a man who pours from a bottle in his right hand—but it dropped on the floor at the right."

Cordero's teeth were white against his beard. "And where did you see this picture, Henry?"

"I saw it going on in Klim's hotel room. I'd been there yesterday morning, you remember. I'd seen the rods at the foot of the bed sprung out, and seen the splashes on the floor. What I hadn't seen at the time was how these might knock Klim's alibi galley-west.

"The clerk called him down for making a racket all night. As a matter of fact, when I thought it over last night, I realized that Klim egged the clerk into doing it —in front of me."

"Do you mean he was clever enough to arrange the whole thing?" Cordero demanded.

Hyer shrugged. "Probably not. He ran into an old friend of his on the way back to the hotel after he had talked to me the night before. He left the friend in his hotel room when he went up to Highbridge—without thinking much about what he was doing. Then he came back and found the friend had raised a rumpus all night. So he realized he had a cover if he could make us believe *he* had made all the noise himself. He fixed himself up to look as if he'd been on an all-night binge, left the watch on Reed's bureau, came and got me—and put on his act."

Cordero was amazed. "Then it *was*—just as we—?"

"They picked up the left-handed friend last night. He said yes, he was in Klim's room all night and what of it?"

Angelica squirmed. "How you know Klim was not left-handed, too, *tío mío?*"

Hyer grinned at her. "The first time he was here, infant, he had to put his hat on the floor to take a glass. He was holding his hat in his right hand. I remembered that."

Madeira appeared in the doorway. "How is the accident ward?" She came to the bed and adjusted Angelica's bandage.

Cordero had risen. His black eyes rested on Madeira, moved to Hyer. They were still bright, but not with amusement.

Hyer said, "I think Angelica needs a new dressing on that bump."

"Oh, no," Madeira began. "It's quite—"

"I think," Hyer said firmly, "Angelica needs a new dressing. Run along, honey, and let Madeira fix you up."

Angelica dutifully swung her bare feet from the bed and slid down.

Madeira said, "We'll be back." She smiled at Cordero, glanced over her shoulder at Hyer, and went out, Angelica trotting beside her.

Cordero closed the door. He said softly, "And now we will complete our bargain, amigo." He drew out a checkbook.

Hyer shook his head.

Cordero's eyebrows lifted. "But you have done your part."

"Not yet."

"Not . . . yet?"

"No," Hyer said, "I'm going to do a little more. It wasn't in the bargain."

Cordero eyed him brightly. "Are you sure you are going to . . . do a little more, Henry?"

"No. But neither are you."

"And Madeira—have you consulted her?"

Hyer said, "No. I wanted to talk to you first."

Cordero turned to the window. He looked down at
the sun-filled gardens for a time. "The check, then—"

"Is out, Cordero."

Cordero laughed quietly. "Because I understand you,
amigo, I will not protest. But there is one matter." He
sat in the window seat. "There is a commitment to Miss
Doudy, I believe."

Hyer nodded. "Five thousand. I'll let you pay that."

Cordero chuckled. He took out his fountain pen.

When Madeira returned, Cordero was standing in the
open door.

"Just leaving," he said. "Will you do the honors, Madeirita?"

From the other room, Jonah called, "Boss, lady to see
you. Want her to— Hey, lady—hey!"

There was a bass growl and a light swift step approaching. In the doorway, Della Doudy said, "Well,
well, just like a class reunion." Her stocky figure was
trim in a black broadcloth suit. Her greenish eyes were
shadowed. There were sharp lines about her small
mouth.

When Madeira and Cordero had left, she gazed after
them speculatively. She came and sat on the edge of the
bed. "Hank," she said in a throaty whisper, "if you say
the word, I'll go to work on Red. Though—" She looked
away. "Right now I'm not exactly up to par."

Hyer patted her hand. He said, "You've done enough.
Here's a souvenir for you." He drew the check from
beneath the coverlet.

Della blinked.

"It'll pay off the mortgage," Hyer said.

"Pay off . . . the mortgage?"

Hyer straightened up. "Do you mean there wasn't any mortgage?"

She skipped back when he reached for the check. "I wouldn't know, darling. I wouldn't know anything about the house." Then her eyes were suddenly grief-stricken. "I never paid the bills, Hank," she whispered.

Cordero's laughter sounded, approaching down the long room. He and Madeira came to the door.

"Hyer," Cordero said, "she's a stubborn *muchacha*."

Madeira flushed. She said, "And I won't be . . . a fee, either."

Hyer grinned. "There's a first-class precedent for it."

Angelica's bare feet pattered down the long room. She ran in at the door, ducked between Cordero and Madeira, and scrambled into bed with Hyer. The bandage was now a becoming white turban.

Della Doudy had been working swiftly at her face. She snapped her compact shut, turned, smiled at Cordero. "I don't suppose," she said huskily, "that anybody's driving uptown."

Cordero looked hard at Hyer. He laughed heartily. "What a coincidence. I'm going that way myself. Henry—" He crossed to the bed, drawing an unwilling Madeira with him. He put out his hand.

Hyer said, "We'll be seeing you."

They shook hands.

Cordero looked down at Madeira. His black eyes were grave. *"Hasta luego,* my dear." . . .

Della Doudy said, "Not that I want to be a nuisance, but I've an appointment at Ciro's. . . . So long, Hank. Make him take care of that ankle, Madeira."

They went out.

Angelica caught at Madeira's dress when Madeira would have followed. "Wait," she commanded.

Madeira sat in the window seat. She looked at the garden. She said, "I will *not* . . . be a fee."

Hyer smoothed Angelica's black hair. He said comfortably, "I can think of worse fates."

The Burke tomcat, creeping along a branch of the ailanthus tree, leaped like a black leopard and stretched himself in the sun on the window ledge. Madeira put out her hand and stroked his glossy back.

"By the way," Hyer said, "there was a Spanish lesson left unfinished last night. You were asking whether Pedro knew something."

Madeira stroked the massive cat thoughtfully. She murmured, *"Qué importa, que Pedro lo sepa ahora."*

Hyer lifted his eyebrow at Angelica.

"She say," Angelica translated, "that Pedro knows now." Then, curiously, to Madeira: *"Qué es lo que sabe Pedro, qué, Tía Madeira?"*

Madeira started. Then she laughed.

Hyer looked at Madeira.

Madeira smiled at the basking panther. "Angelica wonders what it is that Pedro knows, Henry."

"Suppose," Hyer suggested, "you tell us."

"*Pero no hablo las palabras inglesas, Enrique mío* . . ." Madeira began.

Angelica leaned back beside Hyer. "You ask me," she said in disgust, "I think that is just—*cómo se dice*— a way to change one subject."

CPSIA information can be obtained
at www.ICGtesting.com
Printed in the USA
BVHW040929030720
582911BV00014B/265